G000272762

KENT AND EAST SUSSEX UNDERGROUND

by   J. Bradshaw
      N. Caiger
      M. Halpin
      R. Le Gear
      A. Pearce
      H. Pearman
      T. Reeve
      P. Sowan

Members of KENT UNDERGROUND RESEARCH GROUP

MERESBOROUGH BOOKS
1991

Published by Meresborough Books, 17 Station Road, Rainham, Kent. ME8 7RS.

Meresborough Books is a specialist publisher of books about Kent, with some on East Sussex, including the monthly magazine 'Bygone Kent'. A list of titles in print April 1991 will be found at the back of this book.

Printed and bound in Great Britain by
Biddles Ltd, Guildford and King's Lynn.

Contents

Warning

Although holes in the ground can be fascinating places, the reader must remember the following:

1. Many of the sites mentioned in this book are on private land with no public right of access and, in some cases, the exact location has been withheld at the landowner's request. If you wish to visit a site you must ask permission from the landowner first and NEVER trespass. If a site is protected by a fence or other barrier you should NEVER damage it to gain access and must always ensure it is left in a safe condition to prevent accidents to people or animals.

2. If you are exploring the surface of an old mining site, you must beware of possible dangers and keep children and pets under control. Although subsidence of workings is unlikely, it is a possibility that should be borne in mind at all times. NEVER enter the crater of a collapsed shaft since it might open up. With an open shaft, NEVER stand on the edge to look down since the sides may crumble and you could fall down. If you wish to look, lie on the ground facing the shaft and peer over the edge. Although it is tempting, NEVER throw stones down a shaft since they may cause damage and there may be explorers below.

3. Underground exploration can be fascinating but it is also dangerous if not carried out in a safe manner. NEVER go exploring if you are inexperienced — contact the Kent Underground Research Group (see address at back) for advice. A simple code of practice for underground exploration is available free of charge by sending a self-addressed envelope to:
National Association of Mining History Organisations
c/o Peak District Mining Museum, Matlock Bath, Derbys DE4 3NR.

4. In case of need, the South East Cave Rescue Organisation has teams covering Kent and Sussex. To call them out telephone 999 and ask for 'Cave Rescue'.

What lies beneath your feet?

There is something about a hole in the ground that seems to fascinate everyone. Perhaps it is the mystery of the unknown or even a distant memory from our Stone Age ancestors when caves were places of safety. Whatever the reason, there is no shortage of rumours to explain why the hole is there — often there is a rumour with no hole! Churches and large houses with secret passages, underground rivers that flow for miles, smugglers' tunnels — the list is endless. If rumour is to be believed, our ancestors must have been very busy and carried out some feats of engineering to rival the Channel Tunnel! Unfortunately for the romantics, the true purpose of the hole is usually far simpler.

For the first time in one book, truth is separated from rumour and the many kinds of underground feature found in Kent and East Sussex are described. It will surprise many people to learn that this area was one of the oldest mining districts in Britain and many kinds of material were mined. Coal mining is only a relative newcomer and it pales into insignificance compared with the volume and distribution of other mining. Each section gives a general description of the feature and a more detailed account of one or two sites, with Ordnance Survey grid references where possible. Since most of the features were originally excavated in Imperial measurements, distances are usually given in feet rather than metres.

The authors are members of the Kent Underground Research Group which is a branch of the Kent Archaeological Society. No absent-minded professors these, however, since they are part of a new breed of archaeology which is growing nationally — Mining History. Although they are primarily archaeologists and carry out research into old records, they have the skills and equipment of the potholer to explore and survey underground features. The Group produces more detailed publications but this book has been written in easy to understand language to give the reader an introduction to the subject.

There should be something in this book for everyone. If you are interested in local history, it will open up a field of study previously unknown to you. Many villages grew up around mining sites which have now long ceased. As a reference book, it will prove invaluable to researchers or as the basis of school projects. A bibliography of further reading is supplied at the end. If you like walking or touring in the countryside, it will explain many of the peculiar bumps and hollows you come across. For the natural historian, there is a section on plants and animals found underground. Finally, if you are unfortunate enough to be involved with ground subsidence, it will give you an insight into the cause and treatment. From reading this book, you will learn exactly what lies beneath your feet.

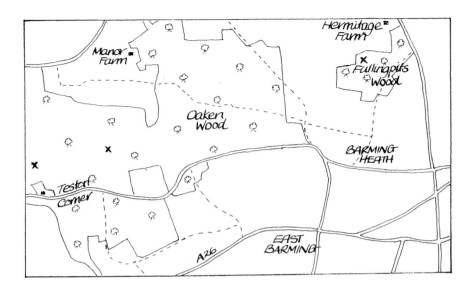

Fig.1 Fullers Earth Pits — Barming

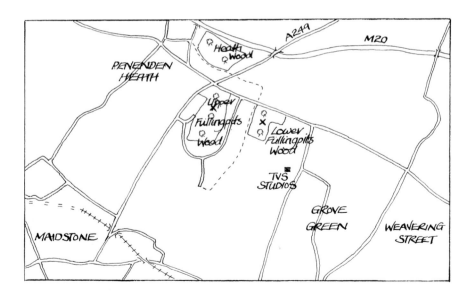

Fig.2 Fullers Earth Pits — Bearsted

6

Fullers Earth Mines

Fullers Earth is a stiff clay with a waxy appearance and it can be either blue, grey or yellow in colour. Like most clays, it is mostly made up of silicon and aluminium but it has traces of many other minerals. Its most useful property is that it is an efficient absorber in powder form. It gets the name from 'Fulling' which is the process of removing grease from woollen cloth. Kent used to be an important wool producer in the 17th century and Fullers Earth was required in great quantities by the Fulling Mills which processed the cloth. It was so valuable once that a law was passed banning its export and a London merchant was heavily fined in 1630 for sending some to Holland. It is now used in face care cosmetics, cat litter and to absorb agents used in Chemical Warfare.

The Kent industry was centred on Maidstone with deposits occurring in an area 9 miles long and 3 miles wide, from West Malling to Leeds. There were once 13 Fulling Mills on the River Loose alone but by 1776 this had been reduced to only 1. The sites of these mills can be traced with a little research and one on the River Len has given its name to Fulling Mill Farm near Leeds (TQ812540). In this area, the Fullers Earth was found in beds up to 7ft thick but it was at a depth of 30ft, being underneath other strata. This made opencast quarrying uneconomical because a vast amount of material would have to be removed first and a large area would be required for the spoil tips. The method employed was to sink wide shafts down to the deposits which, after the Fullers Earth had been extracted, were abandoned. It is not known if horizontal workings led off from the shaft since the roof would require strong support and it was easier to sink another shaft. Underground mining for Fullers Earth did take place in Surrey, however, and it is possible that this was the local practice as well. The whole area would have been pitted with abandoned shafts and a report in 1790 (when the mining had almost died out) stated '. . . there is a pit in work near Maidstone where a large space of ground has been worked over'. There was a brief period of reworking this century near Leeds and Grove Green but these were opencast sites.

In view of the age of the workings, present day remains are scant and consist only of hummocky ground where the shafts have been infilled and planted with trees. Near Barming (Fig. 1), such areas occur at Oaken Wood (TQ703549 & TQ708552) and Fullingpits Wood (TQ728557). Near Grove Green (Fig. 2), they can be found at Lower Fullingpits Wood (TQ777568) and there were also others at Upper Fullingpits Wood (TQ773569) until it was recently built upon. There are probably many more yet to be found. Grove Green was a much worked area and the actual word 'Grove' was an old term for a mine. Much of the area is being built upon and sites are becoming obscured.

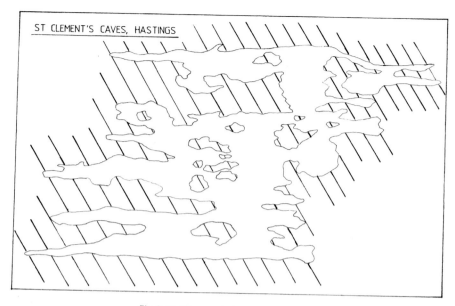

Fig.3 St Clement's Caves — Hastings

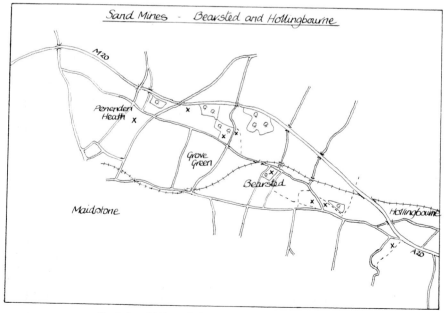

Fig.4 Sand Mines — Bearsted and Hollingbourne

8

Sand & Sandstone Mines

Sand is basically small crystals of silica which, in their pure form, are colourless or white. They are often discoloured by impurities and, whereas the usual colour of sand is yellowish orange, it can be found in just about every colour imaginable. It has had many uses over the years and is especially important nowadays in the building industry as an ingredient of mortar and cement. Before this, however, one common use was in drying ink on documents before blotting paper and the biro were invented. Another use, still important today, was as the raw material for glass making but only the purer forms could be used for this.

The usual reaction of people to a sand mine is that someone is pulling their leg! After all, why mine it when it could be quarried at surface and how could a mine in sand exist without collapsing? The simple answer to the first question is one of economics — where sand deposits were close to the surface then quarrying was easy but where they were deeper it was quicker to mine than remove large amounts of overlying strata. The weight of the latter causes the sand deposits themselves to be compressed at depth and this sand is nothing like the loose sand found on beaches. With careful excavation, the material is surprisingly stable and does not need support.

From a mining point of view, sand is perhaps one of the easiest materials to work in since it can be extracted with pick and shovel. Horizontal passages were driven into the hillside, sometimes from an existing sand pit, and side passages were developed to form a maze of workings. In view of the soft nature of the sand, some skill was called for in shaping the passages so that the cross-section formed an arch with a rounded roof. This spread the weight of overlying strata and meant that extra support was rarely needed. Dimensions varied but passages were normally 6–8ft high. The weak points were at the passage junctions where a greater area of roof was unsupported. Unless these were excavated with great skill, there was a danger of roof collapse and many sand mines have collapsed at such points. Surface remains are almost non-existent since the sand was saleable in its mined form and there was no need for surface treatment.

Perhaps the most well-known sand mines are the St Clement's Caves at Hastings (TQ824097) which are some 3 acres in extent (Fig. 3). There are reports of sand being mined at several sites in the Hastings/ St Leonard's area, one as late as 1858, and some of these are still accessible. Although the St Clement's Caves cannot be accurately dated, a smaller sand mine nearby was excavated before 1783 since a report at

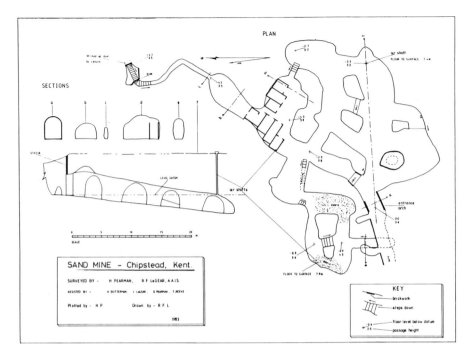

PLAN

SECTIONS

SAND MINE - Chipstead, Kent.

SURVEYED BY - H PEARMAN, R F LeGEAR, A A I S

ASSISTED BY - H BOTTERMAN, J LeGEAR, O PEARMAN, T REEVE

Plotted by - H P   Drawn by - R F L

1983

KEY

brickwork

steps down

floor level below datum

passage height

Fig.5 Sand Mines — Chipstead

that time described how a man and his wife were living in it '. . . having been discharged from the town workhouse for repeated misbehaviour'! They showed some enterprise by guiding visitors around their 'gloomy abode' for a few pence. This seems to indicate that sand mining had taken place here at least in the 18th century since it had ceased by 1783. In 1797 the St Clement's Caves were enlarged to make a temporary hospital for the Worcestershire Militia and in 1827 were developed as a show cave. In World War II the town archives were stored here but it was stated that they were so ravaged by the atmosphere that they would have been better left to the mercies of the enemy! What the sand mined here was used for is unknown but it was possibly for building purposes.

There is a sand mine at Greenwich which is accessible from the garden of a private house. It is believed that sand from here was used locally to make cheap green bottle glass and, although the date of working is unknown, glass making was carried out locally from the 17th century. In 1905, the Greenwich Borough Council stated '. . . We have also visited and examined a complicated and lofty series of tunnels . . . cut into hard sand and extending over a considerable area'. Another report in 1914 described a sand mine in this area '. . . I do not know the

10

exact extent of these excavations but one can wander about in what seems to be a perfect maze of tunnels for a considerable distance'. The presently accessible mine is nothing as great as the reports suggest so, unless there was some exaggeration, there must either be further workings beyond the roof collapses or another mine as yet unfound.

A sand mine at Chipstead (TQ5056) seems to have been associated with a whitening works in the quarry from which it was driven (Fig. 5). It is possible that the fine, white sand was compressed into blocks for cleaning doorsteps. The earliest graffiti in the mine suggest a date of working prior to 1864 and it was worked up until the early 20th century. Subsequent to this it was used as a film store and as an air raid shelter in World War II.

To the north of Maidstone, between Aylesford and Hollingbourne, is found a deposit of particularly fine white sand which was used locally for glass making. It once had such a good reputation that it was sent to London and other parts of England, being used in the manufacture of Ravenscroft's flint glass tableware in the 17th century. Its particular value lay in the lack of impurities and a report in 1834 stated '. . . small white crystals are frequently found in the sand in this parish, they are exceedingly hard and, when polished, are very brilliant; they are known in this neighbourhood by the name of "Bearsted Diamonds".' At Aylesford, it was sufficiently shallow to quarry and the sand pit here produced it for glass making until 1916, since when it has had a more ignominious use in building. Further east, however, it was too deep and it was mined by means of horizontal levels driven into the hillside (Fig. 4).

The first site is in Penenden Heath where there was an old sand pit (TQ772570). It seems very likely that underground levels were driven west from this pit since a serious subsidence occurred at Norman Close (TQ769569) in 1976. A 15ft crater appeared with 'an enormous cavern' below. Another mine is near Newnham Court and the collapsed entrance is at the bottom of a large open pit 300ft long, 240ft wide and 90ft deep (TQ782572). The original date of working was at least the 18th century and perhaps even before. By the mid-19th century it had ceased working but, before then, it had become one of the local attractions for visitors to the area. A report by W. Lamprey in 1834 describes a visit to the mine and, allowing for artistic licence, is a useful insight into the workings. '. . . On our way home from Thurnham we visited the remarkable sand caverns at Newnham Court Farm; and really they are well worthy of notice. These subterranean passages are so long and intricate as to render the assistance of a guide necessary. The boy, who conducted us, said that the length of the various pits exceeded half a mile and that formerly their length was much greater, more than a half

Westerham Ragstone Mine — original size passage. (H. Botterman)

Westerham Ragstone Mine — backfilled passage. (R. Le Gear)

part of them having been filled up by the falling in of earth above, in consequence of the excavators having imprudently cut away the points of support where some of the passages intersected each other. Those persons who intend to descend far into these caverns should provide themselves with a fire box as many have, by their torches being extinguished, been lost in their gloomy and dangerous maze for hours. From these pits, many of the provincial glass manufacturers and stationers in the kingdom are supplied with the fine white sand used in their trades'. The references to the collapses describe a practice known in mining circles as 'pillar-robbing'. When a mine was at the end of its economical life, it often happened that miners obtained fresh material by enlarging passages or whittling away solid pillars left as support. This was a dangerous practice but it meant that material could be excavated quickly and cheaply.

On Hockers Lane (TQ790567) is a disused sand pit from where levels were driven west under Popes Wood. A number of depressions show the collapse of the sand workings underneath this point and a cavity appeared in Hockers Lane itself during drain laying. At Hog Hill in Bearsted (TQ798560) there are a number of craters which are very likely to be collapsed sand workings. A nearby subsidence at the railway station, when several tons of coal disappeared, is probably due to a similar cause. Other craters at Commonwood (TQ807553 & TQ809553) are collapsed levels driven from a nearby sand pit.

At Hollingbourne (TQ823545) there was the entrance to another large sand mine which has now, unfortunately, been almost completely destroyed by the construction of the M20. This mine seems to have been worked to a later date than the one at Newnham Court and it is believed that sand from here was used to make glass for Crystal Palace around 1850. It seems to have closed soon after this but was 're-discovered' in 1898 by a local boy out exploring. The landowner and tenant, Messrs Fremlin and Coveney, opened it to the public as a show cave for 6d a visit and it operated right up to the 1960s. Tool marks were still visible in the walls and the sand contained boulders of iron ore, known locally as 'car stones'. At one point, there was a round shaft in the ceiling leading to a chamber with access to the surface. This is unusual for a sand mine of this type and may have been earlier workings broken into by later mining. The quarry site, from where the entrance went in, is now occupied by a haulage firm.

In some areas, sandstone rock was mined where the surface deposits were too shattered to make large enough blocks for building stone. At Tunbridge Wells (TQ581396) a small shaft was found leading to a large excavated chamber in sandstone. It is possible that this originally supplied building stone and it was made use of in the last war as an air

Chipstead Sand Mine.   (H. Botterman)

Archer Wood Limestone Mine — excavating shaft.   (A. Pearce)

raid shelter. At Cowden (TQ449399) there are four short adits in a sandstone cliff and nearby (TQ581396) is a 50ft adit some 9ft high x 5ft wide. Little is known of their origin but one theory is that the sandstone could have been mined as a furnace lining.

In East Sussex, sandstone was mined in the area of Brightling/Netherfield but the locations are still something of a mystery. The reports of the HM Inspector of Mines between 1895 and the early 1900s list 3 working mines for 'calcareous' sandstone but did not pinpoint where they were. The Blackbrooks Mine and Perch Hill Mine were both owned by Percy Tew of Brightling (later taken over by the mine agent W. Haviland) and it is likely that they were eventually linked underground. The number of miners averaged 10 and the only clue to the location is that they were 7.5 miles from Battle Station! The entrances have not yet been found but they are likely to be between Perch Hill and Willingford (TQ6622). The other site was Woodlands Mine which was originally owned by S. Crowhurst of Netherfield. It seems that he was better at mining than finances since he sold out to C. Egerton of Mountfield in 1899 but stayed on as mine agent. This was a smaller mine with an average of only 4 miners and was said to be 4 miles from Battle Station. Again, the entrance has not yet been found but it could be near Woodlands Farm (TQ719188).

Limestone Mines

Limestone is not generally associated with the South East but there are two types found in Kent and Sussex which have been quarried and mined in the past.

Purbeck Limestone

This is found as a deposit in Sussex where it forms a type of island called an 'inlier' in the middle of other strata. Unlike Carboniferous Limestone, which can be a solid mass over 1,000ft thick, the Purbeck Limestone consists of a number of thin beds of limestone mixed with beds of shale. Collectively they are separated into two main deposits, the shallower 'Greys' and the deeper 'Blues'.

Some of the limestone was used for building purposes in the past when it was given the name of 'Sussex Marble'. A reference in 1860 indicates that it was mined somewhere near Street Green (TQ3918) and Ashdown (TQ4732) but research has yet to reveal the site of these excavations. Although such stone could be quarried, it was often found that surface deposits were too broken up to make large blocks and thus the deeper deposits were obtained by mining.

The largest concentration of limestone mining, however, took place in a rough triangle based on 3 large inliers at Archer Wood (TQ7418), Limekiln Wood (TQ7219) and Rounden Wood (TQ6721). Although some of this was used as roadstone, the majority was burnt to produce agricultural lime to enrich the poor soil of the surrounding area. The earliest method of extraction, and one which was used in places right up to early this century, was to mine the 'Greys' by sinking bellpits. These were similar to deneholes and were described by a contemporary visitor to the area.

'The bell-pits, where of any depth, require 5 men to sink them, two remaining at the windlass while the others work below. A circular shaft, 4ft in diameter, is sunk for 20ft. The quarrymen then commence to bell it out, increasing the diameter with depth, so that eventually the base of a pit, 50 – 55ft deep, is as much as 20ft across. No timbering is necessary unless, as is sometimes the case, the quarrymen proceed to drive out horizontal galleries from the base of the pit. The amount of water in these pits is rarely great and pumps were seldom erected; but pinnocks, or square timber troughs 8 inches square, were laid down from one pit to another and so continued to lower ground.'

The term 'quarrymen' may be confusing to the reader but it was a term used in the South East to describe men who extracted stone either from quarries or mines. Some of the larger stone mines were in fact termed underground quarries and this has caused no end of confusion to researchers looking at old records! The mention of 'pinnocks' is also interesting since it suggests that adjacent bellpits were connected underground, whereas the usual procedure was to keep them separate. In this particular area, the bellpits were usually sunk on the sides of valleys and the collapsed shaft hollows and spoil heaps can still be identified, although now planted around with trees. Examples can be seen to the west of the public footpath which descends to the River Dudwell from Poundsford (TQ638225).

This small-scale mining could not keep pace with the demand for lime and the Earl of Ashburnham, who owned much of the area, devised a revolutionary plan to solve the problem. It was known that better lime could be obtained from the 'Blue' limestone but this was at a greater depth and bellpits could only produce a relatively small amount of limestone for the effort involve. What was required was a larger scale mine but there was no local expertise to operate one. It was easy to sink a shaft and dig out small chambers but special skills were needed to drive levels and excavate limestone in an efficient manner. Thus in 1786 the Earl engaged a mining agent from Derbyshire called Anthony Tatlow. Derbyshire was chosen because of its many lead mines in which the miners had to excavate limestone to get at the ore.

Tatlow was given the job of setting up a system for mining the 'Blue' limestone and burning it to produce sufficient quantities of lime for the area. He selected Orchard Wood (subsequently corrupted to Archer Wood by the Ordnance Survey) for the first mine and teams of Derbyshire lead miners were brought down on contract to develop it. Over the years, a number of miners came back to work in Sussex and, after a year or two, had earned enough to return to buy their own mine. Some, however, carried on for many years and it is possible that descendants of these miners still live in the area. Old records indicate that the Earl took particular trouble to look after the welfare of his miners, something that was not common in those days. As well as housing, he paid for any medical treatment required following accidents in the mine and on several occasions made ex-gratia payments to miners unable to work due to injury. The mine and lime works grew to such a size that they became a small community in their own right with a number of ancillary workers such as road menders, woodcutters, tailors and even a mole catcher!

These miners were fiercely independent and brought with them their system of 'Bargains' for working the mine. They were formed into teams of 2 or 3 and every month would negotiate with the Mine Agent a price per cubic yard of stone brought out of the mine or yard of shaft sunk. This was a gamble and success depended on how easy it was to excavate the limestone, since they were not compensated for bad luck such as hitting unstable areas. The mine was divided into several areas of work, each of which could be bargained for by any of the teams in a process similar to an auction. It suited the Mine Agent because it was in the interests of the teams to extract as much as possible. At the next monthly agreement (or Bargain), either side could negotiate a new price to take account of conditions. If conditions were easy and a great amount was being removed, the Mine Agent might reduce the price for a particular area by offering it to the team willing to work for the least amount. If conditions were difficult and none of the teams was interested, the Mine Agent would be forced to increase the price to allow for the reduction in output and earnings. The system was popular with the mine workers since, despite the risk, large earnings were possible. Two contemporary accounts give an insight into the methods of working.

'. . . they commenced by sinking a main pumping shaft . . . and at a depth of 60ft two levels were driven out to the right and left . . . These, which were called the Wet Levels, constituted the southern boundary of the workings and served to drain the whole of the excavations subsequently made. Two pumps were mounted in the main shaft and were driven by the power derived from an overshot waterwheel. The whole length of the levels was divided into distinct faces of work, by means of galleries driven out at right angles to them, and subsidiary shafts were sunk for the purposes of winding up the stone. A face of work was then gradually carried forward, the miners supporting the roof as they advanced by means of forks or upright timbers with cross props, the limestone being brought to the foot of the shaft along the gallery, while the shale and refuse portion of the stone was thrown back into the 'gobbin' behind. When the distance of the last face of work from the level had reached the limits beyond which the stone could not be drawn with economy, a second face of work was treated in a similar manner and the operation repeated until the whole had been advanced to equal distances from the main Wet Levels. Levels were then driven parallel to the first two, a second series of shafts sunk, and the extraction of the stone recommenced . . . Eventually a third series was sunk . . . Only the 1st, 2nd and 3rd limestones were extracted at first, the 4th being left to form the roof when the 5th and 6th were extracted, the height of the galleries in the first case was 5ft, in the second 4ft . . . With respect to the galleries, care was always taken to keep one side of them, while in use, protected by firm unbroken ground; the hard refuse, stone, etc. was packed in to form a wall upon the other.'

'. . . The shaft by which we descended is 4ft by 5ft, boarded, with ladders for the men to go and return from their work, which is 80ft deep more or less; through this the stone is drawn up in barrels of 5cwt to each, one descending while the other ascends. The whole machinery is moved by a horse and is the same with that generally used in collieries . . . The process in separating the limestone from the solid bed is to blast it with gunpowder; a hole is bored in the rock with an auger; a pricker is put into this whilst the powder is rammed down and, when this part of the operation is finished, the pricker is taken out and a wheat straw filled with powder is put into the place of it, and a small piece of touch paper to the top of the straw, so as to communicate with the powder within, and give time to the workmen to seek a place of safety. When the rock is blown up, the stone rolls down in large blocks, which are broken to a portable size and then conveyed in barrows or little waggons, on roads framed for the wheels to roll along, to the foot of the shaft. A boy fills the bucket, which is drawn up and stacked into square yards.'

The surface of the mine is on a steep valley side and the limestone deposits rose at a lesser angle. Thus the shafts became deeper as the workings proceeded away from the valley bottom, the lower shafts being 60ft deep and the upper ones up to 120ft deep. At these depths, it was impossible to wind stone up by hand and thus a device called a horse gin was used. This was a large horizontal winding drum, pivoted in the centre and turned by a horse. The other interesting reference is to the pumps operated by a waterwheel (the only known use in a mine in the South East) which was fed with water from surface dams. The circular motion of the waterwheel would be converted via a crank to back and forward motion using lengths of connected timber called flat rods. A pivot at the shaft would convert this to up and down motion using flat rods which would operate the pumps at the bottom. Water would be raised in pipes to near the shaft top where it would be directed down a small level to emerge next to the stream. Old references indicate that the waterwheel itself may have been installed underground in a chamber near the top, a procedure used in Derbyshire mines. At surface, the stone from the mining teams was kept in separate places to enable the monthly reckoning to be done. From here it was taken to the nearby kilns to be burnt into lime, using faggots of brushwood cut from the abundant woodlands surrounding the works. The mine produced large quantities of limestone for over 30 years until the miners came up against a geological fault which stopped operations.

There are a number of surface remains identifiable at Archer Wood (Fig. 6) but some are difficult to find since the whole area has now been

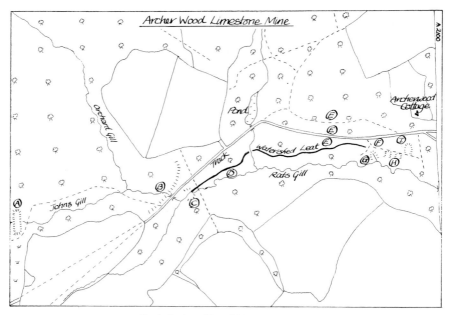

Fig.6 Archer Wood Limestone Mine

planted with trees. Intending visitors should note, however, that the mine area is on private land and permission should be sought before venturing away from the public bridleway. There is a system of three dams (A), (B) and (C) which were used to retain water to operate the waterwheel for pumping. At the second dam, a brick conduit carried water under the track but it has collapsed on the downstream side. From the bottom dam, the leat (D) can be followed as it hugs the contours to retain its level and thus provide a sufficient head of water to operate the waterwheel. In the wood, on either side of the track, are the hollows of the winding shafts (E) which appear to have been filled in. These shafts stop near the top of the valley side where the line of the geological fault can be traced. The pumping shaft (F) is near the valley bottom and the collapsed drainage tunnel (G) is nearby. A deep channel has been cut from its mouth to allow water to flow into the stream. From the pumping shaft, an old track can be followed downstream to where the lime burning was carried out. The remains of two Flame Kilns (H) can be seen to the right of the track and the Tunnel Kiln (I) further down on the left. The history of this interesting mine is being researched in great detail by members of the Kent Underground Research Group and will be covered in one of their future publications.

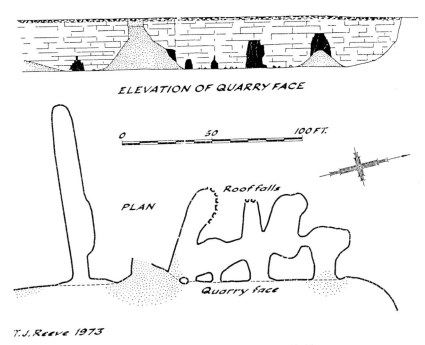

ELEVATION OF QUARRY FACE

0   50   100 FT.

PLAN

Roof falls

Quarry face

T.J. Reeve 1973

Fig.7 Willington Street Stone Mine — Maidstone

Soon after the Archer Wood Mine was set up, the Earl of Ashburnham authorised another one at Dallington Forest. Although this was known as Forest Mine, it actually consisted of three separate adjacent mines at Scotsham (TQ647215), Poundsford (TQ636224) and Westdown (TQ646221). This complex soon came to rival Archer Wood for output and it is believed that it carried on long after Archer Wood ceased operations. The lime produced by the Earl's mines soon came to earn a favourable reputation for quality and it was actually shipped from Hastings to London where it was in demand for making mortar.

The success of the lime works soon tempted the Earl's neighbours to start similar schemes and there are references to other limestone mines in the area. Although the exact locations have yet to be identified, they are at Willingford (TQ6522), Brightling (TQ6721), Darwell Road (TQ7119) and Hurst Green (TQ7327). It is not known if these mines were on the same scale as those of the Earl of Ashburnham but skilled miners would certainly have been available who had obtained their experience at the Earl's mines.

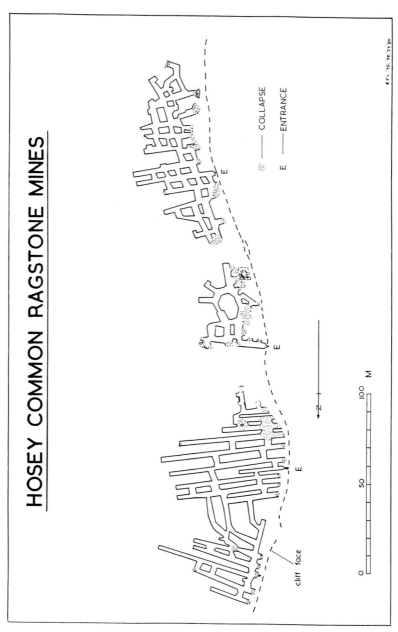

Fig.8 Hosey Common Ragstone Mines

Ragstone

This deposit occurs in the Greensand Beds and is variously described as a 'limey' sandstone or a 'sandy' limestone (the latter term being more correct). It is found in the area around Maidstone and Westerham and was used in the past as a building stone. Local deposits were in fact used by the Romans to construct the walls of London and it was later used in the Tower of London, St Paul's Cathedral and Rochester Castle. Large quarries existed around Maidstone and it is known to have been mined in at least three locations in the vicinity of Mote Park, viz. TQ778542, TQ785541 and TQ786543. These seem to have been underground extensions of surface quarries but the latter two sites (Fig. 7) have now been built upon. None of the mines are believed to be accessible now.

The mines at Hosey Common, Westerham (TQ454531) are believed to date from the 17th century but little is known of their history at present. Again, they produced building stone and this was used for Westerham Church. They lie on the side of a shallow valley and the area is now heavily wooded. Four separate sets of workings have been identified (Fig. 8) and it is believed that more exist but are inaccessible due to roof falls. The mines were worked on the pillar and stall principle and the original passages were up to 7ft high by 8ft wide. Transport underground was by sledges and excavation in the floor has revealed sledge marks with a gauge of 14.5ins. At some time in the past, however, the passages were backfilled with waste rock and this has only left a gap of a few feet. It is believed that this was carried out at a time when the price for the stone dropped drastically and the only economical way of working was to extract the best quality stone only. This meant that a great deal of poorer quality rock was no longer required and it was more convenient to stack it in abandoned passages rather than carry it out of the mine.

These mines have suffered several roof falls in the past and they are a maze of passages so exploration by inexperienced persons is not recommended. In addition, they are the most important hibernation sites for bats in S.E. England so the entrances have been grilled to prevent unauthorised access.

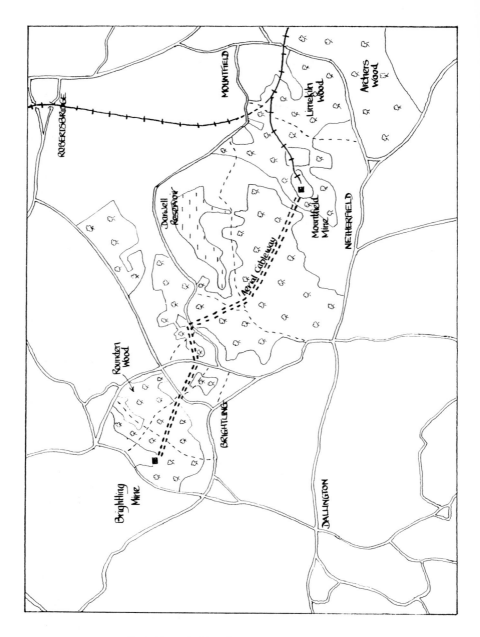

Fig.9 Mountfield and Brightling Gypsum Mines

Gypsum Mines

Gypsum is in great demand by the building industry to make plaster and plaster board, both essential for internal walls. In its natural state, it is a rock found in seams which are several feet thick and it is crushed into powder to make the finished product. In this country most of the mining is carried out by British Gypsum Ltd who have mines in the Northern Pennines, Midlands and Sussex.

The only surviving working mines in Sussex trace their history back to a meeting of the British Association for the Advancement of Science, held at Brighton in 1872. The geologists at this gathering resolved to sink a borehole, as deep as could be made, through the oldest rocks visible at the surface in South East England. These were the Purbeck Beds at Limekiln Wood near Mountfield (TQ720194). A subscription was raised and it is likely that the project attracted more than scientific interest and support as there was a possibility that the coal seams worked in Somerset and Belgium might also be found at this spot.

After a number of accidents and false starts, the borehole eventually reached a depth of 1,905ft in 1876 when the drilling rods broke and the project was stopped. No coal was found but there was a greater than expected thickness of younger rocks. The investment of £6,000 was not devoid of commercial interest, however, since several thick seams of gypsum had been found at depths between 130–160ft. The Sub-Wealden Gypsum Co. Ltd was formed on 10th May 1876 and mining commenced by sinking a shaft about 60yds from the borehole (Fig. 9). Progress was difficult and slow on account of the isolated location, until a railway link had been constructed to the main line at Robertsbridge.

An early description of the operations in 1881 refers to beds of gypsum from 6–7ft high, into which headings of a similar width were driven by drilling and blasting. These were all connected by a network of underground rails to carry the gypsum to the shaft bottom, where it was hoisted to the surface by a steam winding engine. During the 1880s, the mine was a small but significant contributor to the total U.K. production, raising about 8,000 tons per annum with a value (at the mine) of about £9,000.

A curious result of the opening of this mine was that the H.M. Inspector of Mines could no longer ignore the South East of England, as had been the case up to this point. This was hardly surprising in view of the national publicity arising from the experimental boring, laying of a railway track and creation of a deep mine. All underground workings for minerals, other than coal or iron, had been subject since 1872 to inspection and other requirements under the Metalliferous Mines

Regulations Act of that year. Although bureaucratic tidiness had placed the south-eastern counties in a mining inspection district, they had been tagged onto that for Manchester & Ireland! It was not until 1882 that the Inspector started to take a serious interest in Sussex, Surrey and Kent, despite the fact that a number of small mines had been at work for many years.

In 1890, Sussex was transferred to the North Wales & Isle of Man District, under an exceptionally able and diligent Inspector who made a point of keeping a very close eye on what were at times very slapdash methods. During the 1890s, the gypsum mine's workforce gradually rose from 15 to 27 men underground and from 22 to 60 on the surface. This reflected the development of a processing plant at the mine, whose main market was plaster for building purposes. Output of gypsum during the same period increased from 6,000 to 18,000 tons per annum but the value only increased from £3,000 to £6,000, from which it appears that the market price of gypsum was in decline and the mine's profits questionable. Perhaps for these reasons the original company was wound up in 1903. After a 'short stoppage' of production in 1906 – 7, during which working methods were thoroughly overhauled, mining resumed on a larger (and presumably more profitable) scale.

Production increased again immediately after the Second World War and the winding shaft was replaced by a sloping adit with an electrically operated railway system. In the early 1950s there was further development, with the opening of a second larger mine at Brightling (TQ676217). In view of the scenic value of the surrounding countryside and of the unsuitability of local roads for heavy freight, the two mines were linked by an overhead cableway (Fig. 9) generally well-hidden amongst the trees. This allowed gypsum from the Brightling Mine to be taken to the processing plant at Mountfield Mine and the cableway has recently been replaced by an updated conveyor belt system. Gypsum is sent away from the plant by rail for similar reasons.

The mines today are extensive, with pillar and stall operations on a scale several times larger than the 6ft x 7ft tunnels made in earlier years. The modern miners travel to their working places underground by landrover and the newly-blasted gypsum is extracted using enormous scraper-loader machines, crushing plant and conveyor belts. Surveyed reserves of gypsum appear to guarantee the enterprise for the foreseeable future.

Flint Mines

Many sites in Kent and Sussex (especially deneholes) have mistakenly been called flint mines, usually when there is a hole for which no purpose is known. This is an understandable mistake because flint nodules can be seen in the chalk and it is assumed that these were the purpose of the excavation. The problem with flint nodules, however, is that they are no good for making large implements since the process of 'knapping' them into shape left many waste flakes. Thus an average sized flint nodule would only produce a relatively small tool such as a scraper or arrowhead. For the larger flint axes, it was necessary to use a deposit called 'Tabular' flint which was formed in massive seams from which big pieces could be broken off. Since such deposits are not common at the surface, this caused the axe-making industry to be concentrated in just a few locations and it became a specialist art. It seems, however, that the axes were only roughly shaped and it was left to the 'customer' to finish and polish them. The axe makers traded their wares for food, etc. and their axes were exported to a wide surrounding area.

Originally, the tabular flint would have been taken from surface outcrops where it was exposed naturally and such surface sites have been found in Kent at Crayford, Northfleet, Frindsbury, Cuxton and Bapchild, as well as Slindon Park in Sussex. Once surface deposits had been worked out, Neolithic Man had to resort to mining if he wished to continue using the site and the well-known flint mines at Grimes Graves in Norfolk have over 300 shafts in an area of 34 acres. Techniques varied according to the stability of the chalk and some 'mines' are little more than deep pits up to 20ft deep and wide. Others are proper mines where a shaft was sunk to the flint seams and horizontal galleries driven off from the bottom. Deer antlers were used as picks to prise out the flint and it is possible that the chalk underneath was undercut to cause the tabular flint to crack and fall away. Stone axes have also been found which were probably used to break up the chalk.

Despite claims to the contrary, no proof of flint mining has been discovered in Kent and it is likely that sufficient surface sites were available to supply the need. Sussex, however, has a number of flint mines and sites have been found at Harrow hill (TQ081100), Blackpatch Hill (TQ094089), Church Hill (TQ112083), Cissbury (TQ137079) and Windover Hill (TQ545035). Sites at Stoke Down and Lavant may also be flint mines. Cissbury, Harrow Hill and Windover Hill have been dated between 2,500 and 2,000 B.C. and the other two sites seem to have taken over from them and continued into the Bronze Age. Little can be seen today apart from rough mounds.

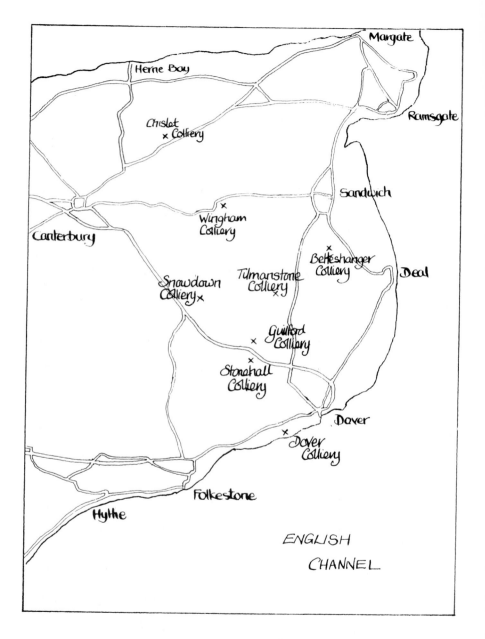

Fig.10 The Kent Coalfield

Coal Mines

During the 19th century a number of geologists suggested that coal might exist in the South East. A bed of lignite had been discovered in 1801 near Heathfield but this was of poor quality and was only sufficient to keep a local blacksmith going for two weeks. The existence of coal mines in France and Belgium suggested that coal might be found at a greater depth and boreholes were sunk at various locations in the hope of finding rich coal deposits. These were at Bexhill (1804), Rotherfield (1806), Maresfield (1806), Horsham (1813) and Mountfield (1872) but it was only at Dover that enough coal was found to make mining operations worthwhile.

The Dover borehole was commenced in 1886 by the Kent Coalfields Syndicate Ltd on the site of the old Channel Tunnel works at Shakespeare Cliff, 3 miles west of Dover (TR295393). It was stopped in 1893 at a depth of 2,230ft, having passed through 1,190ft of the Coal Measures and proved the existence of several coal seams. As a result of this, it was decided to sink a shaft down to mine the coal, especially a 4ft seam at a depth of 2,172ft. Shaft No. 1 (Brady Pit) was commenced near the borehole in July 1896. It was 17ft in diameter and rapidly passed through the Chalk, Chalk Marl and Gault Beds until it reached the Lower Greensand Beds in October at a depth of 366ft. At this point, so much water seeped into the shaft that it had to be abandoned.

The problem was that the Greensand Beds were pervious and contained a great amount of water which was held in position by the impervious Gault Beds above. As soon as the shaft pierced this cover, the water was released from pressure and was forced up the shaft. This is the principle of artesian wells and a similar effect can be obtained by placing an empty bucket into water and piercing a hole in the bottom — water will be forced into the bucket from below until it reaches the level of the surrounding water. Since the Greensand Beds here are at an angle, the level of the 'surrounding water' will correspond to the highest point that the Beds rise to in the area. This happens to be under the English Channel and so the Greensand will never run dry! In this case, water rose to within 40ft of the top of the shaft as it also had in the borehole.

Shortly after Shaft No. 2 (Simpson Pit) was started nearby and was slightly wider at 20ft diameter. Having experienced water problems with the first shaft, the precaution was taken of putting down 15ft boreholes from the shaft bottom as it was sunk in order to give advance warning of flooding. At 10.55pm on 6th March 1897, a team of 14 men

Tilmanstone Colliery early this century. (A. Ritchie)

Guilford Colliery early this century. (A. Ritchie)

were working in the shaft bottom when the top bed of the Lower Greensand was struck. Initially there was no sign of water and there was no indication of danger until a few minutes later, when it was found that the sand was wet. Suddenly, water shot up into the shaft from underneath and only 6 men were able to escape by climbing up the iron rings supporting the timber lining. The hoppit (large bucket) was at the surface being emptied when cries were heard from below. It could only hold 3 men at a time and was quickly lowered twice to rescue survivors clinging to the shaft walls. Two men went down in the hoppit a third time but the water had risen 80ft up the shaft and they could see no more survivors. It took over a month before workers were able to pump out the shaft and recover the 8 bodies and work was suspended. It was subsequently found that the water level in the bore-hole and Brady Pit had dropped 127ft at the time of the accident. The probable explanation is that, under a head of about 265ft of water from both the nearby borehole and Brady Pit, sufficient pressure was exerted on the water in the Lower Greensand to burst through the few feet of hard sandstone and clay that formed the bottom of the shaft.

Despite this disaster, sinking later continued but Dover Colliery earned a reputation for costing a lot of money with little result. It was not until 1912 that the first (and only) consignment of coal was sent from the mine and this was only 120 tons! There was a big celebration to commemorate this but there were strong rumours that the coal had actually been brought from elsewhere to impress disillusioned share-holders. Needless to say, the colliery did not last much longer although iron ore was extracted for a short time.

The turn of the century saw an enormous amount of activity in East Kent and over 40 boreholes were sunk to discover reserves of coal. Unfortunately for the reputation of the coalfield, a great many com-panies were set up of dubious intention and many shareholders lost money in speculative ventures. The kingpin at that time was Arthur Burr and he was associated with over 20 separate companies, many of which went into liquidation. His speciality was to be elected 'manager for life' of these companies and he transferred money between them as if they were all one (which effectively they were!). It seems amazing that he continued to persuade shareholders to invest in his schemes but people seemed hypnotised by the prospect of great profits to be made. When Burr was eventually make bankrupt, the judge made several scathing comments about his activities and called him a rogue. By acquiring the mineral rights to most of the coalfield, Burr's companies effectively retarded development since they did not have enough capital to develop mines in a proper manner. The piecemeal develop-ment ended with nationalisation in 1947 when the National Coal Board took over.

Underground in Kent coal mine. (A. Ritchie)

First load of coal wound out of Snowdown Colliery. (A. Ritchie)

In the event, the only collieries which were anything like productive (Fig. 10) were Betteshanger (TR336530), Chislet (TR209619), Snowdown (TR247512) and Tilmanstone (TR288505). Others were sunk at Guilford (TR280469), Stonehall (TR271456) and Wingham (TR253569) but these never produced coal. Before the bubble burst, there were grandiose schemes for many more collieries as well as complete new towns for the workers. The port of Richborough was intended to be the focal point of a lucrative export trade and plans were made for associated steel industries. Had these plans come to fruition, the countryside of East Kent would have been another South Wales or Lancashire. At the time of writing, the only working colliery left is at Betteshanger and its future is unknown. The usual policy of British Coal is to completely landscape coal mines when abandoned. As a result, few surface remains still exist and the Tilmanstone Colliery has been completely flattened. There are, however, still some remains of the private Guilford Colliery and the old engine house can be seen today in the farmyard which occupies the site.

Depth of Coal Mine Shafts

Betteshanger No. 1	2,162ft
Betteshanger No. 2	2,426ft
Chislet North	1,470ft
Chislet South	1,467ft
Dover 'X'	520ft
Dover 'Y'	1,632ft
Dover 'Z'	1,632ft
Guilford No. 1	306ft
Guilford No. 2	1,272ft
Guilford No. 3	1,272ft
Snowdown No. 1	262ft
Snowdown No. 2	3,083ft
Snowdown No. 3	2,994ft
Stonehall West	273ft
Stonehall East	273ft
Stonehall North	75ft
Tilmanstone No. 1	1,590ft
Tilmanstone No. 2	3,168ft
Tilmanstone No. 3	3,139ft
Wingham East	50ft
Wingham West	150ft

There was another coal mine at Cobham near Rochester (TQ674696) but this mined a poor quality brown lignite which outcropped at the surface in a small valley. For a number of years it had been opencasted by the landowner Lord Darnley who used it for domestic purposes at Cobham Hall. In 1947, however, an unlikely combination of a mining engineer, solicitor and café owner set up the Cobham (Kent) Mining Co. Ltd to mine it on a commercial scale. The mine was visited by the London Speleological Group who have left us with this record:

'. . . There are two drifts driven at right angles to the gulley. The West drift has been blocked by a fall but the other — the lifeline of the workings — is intact. This particular gallery extends for a distance of 55yds and has three working faces leading from it. The dip of the workings is 1:12 with a seam 6ft thick, no difficulty is experienced in working. At present, black lignite is being mined which resembles poor quality bituminous coal but some good bituminous coal has been found and larger strikes are expected soon. The overburden at the face is 60ft. Haulage is by tubs, one at a time, running on a single tramway and hauled by a diesel winch. Illumination is with acetylene lamps and all hewing is done by hand. Difficulty is being experienced with water which, besides flooding the workings, causes minor roof falls, made more likely by the fact that the roof is of shaly Woolwich and Reading Beds. However, the water is being kept under control with a petrol driven pump. With a working strength of 5 men, 3 at the face and 2 at the bank, the output per man per shift is 5.5 tons — 80 tons a week. The tonnage of ore available has yet to be proved but it is known that the seam extends 300yds to the East and a further seam of lignite is believed to exist 60ft below the present workings. It is proposed to drive an adit from the lower end of the gulley to the mine sump and so drain off the water. If the present labour force can be increased, an output of 150 tons a week is anticipated.'

This proposed expansion never happened since, as well as the water problems, the company was having difficulty in selling the product and encountered methane as the gallery was driven deeper into the hillside. It was eventually wound up in 1953 and the entrances were blown in. When the nearby A2 road was upgraded, the new carriageway passed over the site of the engine house and offices and little trace remains today. Opposite the Laughing Water Motel, about 100yds into the wood, a number of deep depressions exist which are the result of the collapsed workings.

Iron Mines

Iron is found in many places in Britain and the type found in the South East is called Ironstone, which is an iron oxide varying in colour between yellow and red. A poor quality variety known as 'Carstone' is found in the sandy Folkestone Beds but better quality ore occurs as nodules in the Ashdown Beds and Wadhurst Clay. During the Iron Age (about 200 B.C.), carstones were obtained from surface workings in Kent and Sussex but, as the Weald was explored, the better quality ores were discovered and exploited. Settlements of ironworkers grew up around the mine sites and several have been identified at Crowhurst, Dallington and Ticehurst in Sussex. More important sites were defended with hill forts such as those at Saxonbury and West Hoathly. During the Roman occupation, the Weald was the main source of iron for military and civilian use and the slag from the smelting process was used in road foundations.

The ore was originally extracted by opencast methods in bowl-shaped pits, up to 60ft wide and 45ft deep. They were infilled upon abandonment but many can be seen today as waterlogged depressions. Later techniques involved sinking shafts up to 7ft wide and 35ft deep down to the iron deposits (Fig. 11), the bottom being widened as much as stability would allow. The word 'Mine' was actually the local expression for the iron ore itself (the excavation being called 'Pit') and a number of Minepit Shaws still exist, referring to small copses planted over the sites of iron mines. The smelting of iron was by the process known as the 'Bloomery' method in which alternate layers of iron ore and charcoal were built up, set alight and then covered with clay to form a primitive oven. Bellows were used to fan the flames and the end product was a malleable ball of impure iron which could be hammered to shape. A researcher, E. Straker, has identified over 100 such sites in the Weald. With its abundant supply of ore and charcoal, the area continued to be a principal centre of the British iron industry and in 1253 the Sheriff of Sussex was called upon by Royal Decree to furnish the Army with 30,000 horseshoes and 60,000 nails.

In Tudor times, the industry was revitalised by the introduction of the blast furnace from the Continent. In this, the ore and fuel were continually added to the top of the furnace and molten iron was drawn off from the base for casting. These were not always popular with the inhabitants as is shown by a complaining letter regarding a wood near Westwell, Kent (TQ9850), sent by Archbishop Parker to Queen Elizabeth in 1570. '. . . Sir Richard Sackville intends to erect iron mills, which plague, if it should come into the country, I fear will breed much grudge and

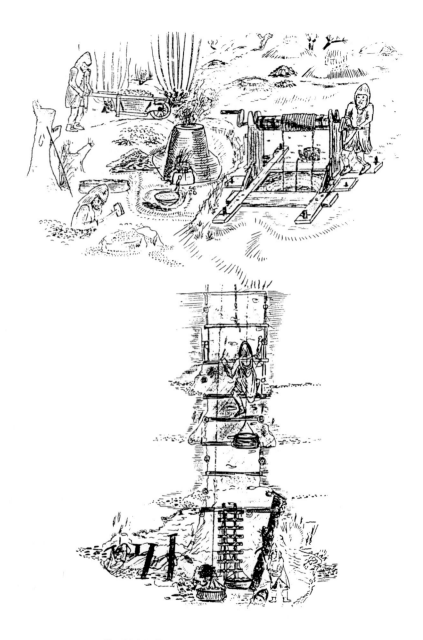

Fig.11 Mediaeval Iron Mine and Bloomery

desolation'. Despite opposition, the Weald became famous for its manufacture of cannons and a report in 1653 lists 27 furnaces and 42 forges.

With the increase in technology, smelting became based at certain locations and iron ore was brought there from surrounding mines. We gain an insight into mining operations in the early 18th century from a contemporary report.

'The price we give for it (iron ore) here is 12d a load which is 12 bushels if they take it as it ariseth, but if they take only the best sorts of oare, which we call veins, and leave the worst, they call 'Eleven Foot Pitty' and 'Bottom', they are paid 18d a load . . . The owner of the ground alloweth 2d for throwing in the Clayes, and also levelling the pits . . . and then the ground will look as well than before the oare was dug.'

It goes on to advocate the extraction of the lowest veins first and then the upper veins, since otherwise water from the upper veins would drown out the lower ones before they could be extracted. A later report says that the ore was worked by means of bell pits of some 6ft diameter at the surface, widening at the bottom. They were generally shallow, rarely more than 20ft deep, and sometimes connected by levels. Great numbers of these pits remain in the woods, generally full of water. On the pasture fields they have been partly filled up, and here the surface very much resembles that produced by 'day-falls' near the outcrop of a worked out coal seam. In view of the number of iron mining sites in Sussex and parts of Kent, it is difficult to pick out a few representative samples. Those who wish to learn more, however, are recommended to read the excellent publication 'Iron Industry of the Weald'. This covers the methods of working and includes a gazetteer of sites.

By the end of the 18th century, the local industry was in decline through a combination of lack of wood and the competition from Wales and the North with their abundant coalfields. The last furnace at Ashburnham (TQ685171) closed in 1809 and a contemporary report describes the state of the industry at that time.

'. . . It was the last furnace in use in Sussex and Kent and was brought abruptly to a close in consequence of the intoxicated habits of the foundry men. By neglecting the proper mixture of chalk, etc. with the ore, the flux did not separate as it should have done to run off and it remained a mass from which the iron could not be drawn off to be run into the pigs (moulds) for the forge. The blasting was of necessity stopped and no attempt made afterwards to renew the work. It was the habit of the gin drinking that brought the work to a premature close before the iron was all worked up.'

Iron mining was not quite dead, however, and there was a brief revival at Snape Wood near Wadhurst (TQ633302) when deposits were found during construction of the railway. This was described in 1875.

'The mine was commenced in August 1857 and abandoned in September 1858; the ore was sent into Staffordshire. The ironstone was worked on both sides of the railway, just west of the 53rd milestone, by levels and cross cuts. On the north side of the railway only one bed was worked, this was 1ft 9ins thick, underlain by hard sandstone. The roof is sometimes bad and required timbering. On the south side of the railway two beds were worked, only one of which could be examined . . . as the level contained much water; this bed was 2ft thick. In this level the ground was softer and required more timber. The beds of ironstone were very irregular but were found to be better on the south than on the north side; in both cases, however, the beds died out suddenly and re-appeared at intervals. Several shafts have been sunk from the higher ground. The ore, a clay-ironstone, was sometimes calcined on the spot. A great deal of raw ore still lies by the side of the railway.'

The main gallery of the mine was about 450ft long, 4ft 6ins wide and 6–8ft high. Wrought iron rails were laid in the gallery which is not far below the surface. Two entrances were filled in to make a road and the remaining post-war shaft filled after two Boy Scouts were temporarily stuck down it. The spoil heaps can still be seen but there are no open entrances. A small inn by the railway, the Miners' Arms, has been converted into a private dwelling. Iron was also mined for a short time from Dover Colliery (see under 'Coal Mines').

Deneholes

In 1570 the historian William Lambarde wrote in his 'Perambulations of Kent':

'. . . There are to be seen . . . near this town . . . sundry artificial caves or holes in the earth, whereof some have ten, some fifteen and some twenty fathoms in depth: at the mouth (and thence downward) narrow, like the tunnell of a chimney or passage of a well: but in the bottom large, and of great receipt: insomuch as some of them have sundry rooms (or partitions) one within another, strongly vaulted, and supported with pillars of chalk, and, in the opinion of the inhabitants, these were in former times digged, as well for the use of the chalk towards building, as for to marle their arable lands therewith . . .'

Lambarde was describing the excavations which have become known as deneholes. The term denehole (or dene-hole, dene hole or danehole) is semi-modern in usage, the earlier writers on the subject describing them as 'pits'. The particular holes mentioned above were in Stankey Wood near Bexley and Crayford (TQ506728).

A denehole is an underground structure consisting of a number of small chalk caves entered by a vertical shaft. The chalk uplands of Kent once contained many hundreds, if not thousands, of deneholes of various types and the origins and purpose of these man-made excavations were the subject of intense interest and debate in the latter 19th century. Some of the open shafts were visited by Victorian historians who descended into the caves and produced drawings and surveys of varying quality. One of the most useful to the modern researcher was the eminent antiquarian F.C.J. Spurrell's paper 'Dene-holes and Artificial Caves with Vertical Entrances', published in the Archaeological Journal for 1881 and 1882.

At this time, many theories were put forward to explain why these structures were excavated, varying from Druids' temples, flint mines and ancient hiding places to elaborate animal traps. By the end of the 19th century, however, opinion had polarised between ancient grain storage pits and chalk mines. It seems that the chalk mine idea was not too popular despite Lambarde's observations 200 years before. After all, a simple chalk mine is not as romantic as a Druid's lair or a neolithic grain store! In the early 1950s, a very active and competent amateur archaeologist, J.E.L. Caiger, brought the eye of a professional engineer and surveyor to bear on the denehole controversy. His investigations over many years included detailed surveys, surface and underground excavations and documentary research which added greatly to our store of knowledge.

Denehole at Bexley — note foot holes in shaft. (R. Le Gear)

Descending denehole shaft on wire ladder. (M. Jack)

From Caiger's pioneering work and subsequent investigation and research by the Kent Archaeological Society and Kent Underground Research Group, it can now be stated that deneholes are no more than small chalk mines. The vast majority were sunk to obtain an unpolluted supply of chalk to spread on the surrounding fields as a fertiliser. The method had much to recommend it as a small shaft at the edge of a field would not interfere with farming operations and could easily be blocked when mining ceased. Opencast extraction would, on the other hand, have meant the removal of a thick overburden and the loss of precious arable land. This method of winning chalk was in use in Kent before the Roman conquest and continued in varying forms, with a brief break in the 15–16th centuries, until the turn of the present century. In fact, whilst the archaeologists were arguing as to the age and use of these mysterious holes in the 1880s, similar excavations were still being dug, often in the same areas as their older counterparts!

To modern eyes, it is puzzling why a shaft would be sunk when chalk might occur almost at surface nearby. The simple answer to this is that the shallow chalk was probably not on the farmer's property since land tended to be owned in much smaller parcels then. In addition, the old roads were in very bad condition and it was too difficult to carry heavy loads any distance in a cart. Another reason for deep extraction was that farmers preferred chalk from a depth, saying that it was 'fatter'. This has some truth in that chalk near the surface usually has various elements such as magnesium leached out.

Deneholes/Chalkwells

Although there are many variations of the basic denehole ground plan, there are two distinct types (Fig. 12). Within the two main types there exist variations in shape depending on the mining techniques employed and there are also regional differences as separate mining teams developed their own particular style. The first (and regarded as earlier) type consists of a narrow shaft, about 3ft in diameter, sunk through the overlying strata (usually Thanet Sand) until the chalk was reached. Footholds were cut on opposite sides of the shaft so that miners could climb in and out without a ladder. After reaching the chalk, a number of chambers were excavated and these were often in two sets of three to give a double clover leaf or trefoil pattern. This type was being dug up until the late 14th century and is usually referred to as the true denehole.

The second type is generally known as a chalkwell (or draw well) and was sunk in areas where the chalk was overlain by a heavy soil such as clay. The shaft of these types is wider, from 4–6ft in diameter, and the chambers consist of between 2–4 roughly cut caves radiating from the

Base of denehole shaft — such features are often used to dump rubbish! (T. Reeve)

Looking up denehole shaft — remains of brick dome at top. (T. Reeve)

base of the shaft. This type was being dug from the 17th century right up to the beginning of this century.

Uses of Chalk

The vast majority of deneholes were dug to obtain a supply of chalk to spread on the local fields as a top dressing, a process known as chalking or marling. Chalk is lost or 'leached' from the soil at a rate depending on rainfall and soil texture and an application of chalk will replace the lost calcium. On clay based soils, marling will help to break up the heavy soil and will assist drainage. On acidic soils, such as those lying on Thanet Sand, chalk will neutralise or 'sweeten' it. Chalk was traditionally mined and spread on the fields in late autumn so that the nodules of chalk would be broken down and powdered by the winter frosts, ready to be ploughed into the soil in the following spring. The use of chalk as a fertiliser has been known for many centuries and the Roman historian, Pliny the Elder, wrote in 70 A.D. about the ancient British mining it for this purpose.

'. . . the chalk is sought from a deep place, wells being frequently sunk to 100ft, narrowed at the mouth, the vein spreading out within as in mines. This is the kind most used in Britain. It lasts for 80 years and there is no instance of anyone who has put it on twice in his lifetime . . .'

Old Norman leases often contained covenants to ensure that chalk was regularly applied to the land and a statute of Henry III in 1225 gave every man the right to sink a marl pit on his own land. Although the primary use of chalk from deneholes and chalkwells was for agricultural use, the excavated material could be, and was, used for building and for road making and repairs. It is also possible that some of the smaller brickfields obtained a supply of chalk from chalkwells rather than excavating a quarry or larger chalk mine. Some were associated with lime kilns since lime mortar was used to bond together bricks before cement was invented.

Mining Methods — Deneholes

The shaft was sunk as close as possible to the field boundary so that any future subsidence would not interfere with ploughing operations. Many deneholes can be found in distinct association with earthwork boundaries. In some areas, the miners would have a problem if the Thanet Sand, which is relatively stable, was overlain with a loose material such as gravel. If this layer of loose and friable material was less than 2ft deep, the area of the shaft would be cleared of gravel before shaft sinking commenced. This would prevent the loose material running in on top of them as the shaft was sunk. This method of making the shaft top safe was used in the Bexley area, particularly at the site of

Fig.12 Some Denehole Types

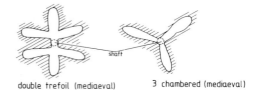

double trefoil (mediaeval)   3 chambered (mediaeval)

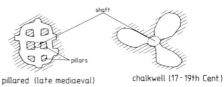

pillared (late mediaeval)   chalkwell (17-19th Cent.)

RFL

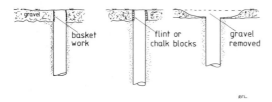

basket work   flint or chalk blocks   gravel removed

RFL

Fig.13 Deneholes — Shaft Construction

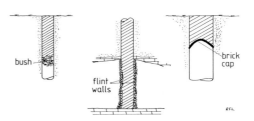

bush   flint walls   brick cap

RFL

Fig.14 Deneholes — Shaft Filling

Stankey Wood. If the layer of gravel was too thick to be easily cleared away, the miners would line the top of the shaft with a wicker basket type of construction to prevent run-ins (Fig. 13). Another method was to line the shaft top with roughly squared flints or chalk blocks (steining) as was found in a denehole near Swingfield (TR224439).

Once the spot for the shaft had been chosen and cleared as necessary, it would be sunk vertically through the Thanet Sand, using the hauling rope and basket as a plumb line, until the chalk was reached. After leaving about 3ft for roof thickness, two opposing headings were commenced as the start of the usual double trefoil plan. Some early writers marvelled at the symmetry of the two sets of chambers and the care with which they were constructed, comparing them with the building of cathedrals, etc. The excavators had in fact developed the most efficient shape for extracting the maximum amount of chalk with the minimum of effort. They were constructed with care to ensure stability and reduce the risk of roof falls. The excellent finish and obvious knowledge of mining techniques indicates that most dene-holes were dug by groups of professionals hiring out their services to the local farmers.

A mining team would have consisted of three men. One would work below ground cutting out the chalk using a short headed iron pick, working forward in a series of steps or 'benches'. These abandoned benches have, in the past, led to tales of Druids' altars, etc! The chalk was hauled to the surface in a basket by the miner's two companions, using a small windlass mounted over the shaft. The length of the under-ground chamber was determined by the friction generated by the hauling rope on the chalk at the base of the shaft. When the majority of double trefoil deneholes were being dug, the wheelbarrow had yet to be invented so transporting the chalk for any distance underground would have been a problem. The miner thus filled the basket at the working face (Fig. 15) and, when the above friction became too great for the surface workers to haul it up, the end of the chamber was trimmed and that part of the mine considered finished. Most deneholes have deep grooves visible at the base of the shaft where the hauling ropes have cut into the soft chalk.

When excavations had ceased in the denehole, a bush or tree stumps were thrown down the shaft (Fig. 14). These would invariably jam part way down and the shaft was then backfilled to surface. Many denehole sites are now in woods or long narrow copses (known locally as 'Shaves' or 'Shaws') where farmers have planted trees in the past to isolate the area. Very few deneholes are still accessible but one at Darenth Wood (TQ578725) can be entered by sliding down a slope where one of the chambers has collapsed.

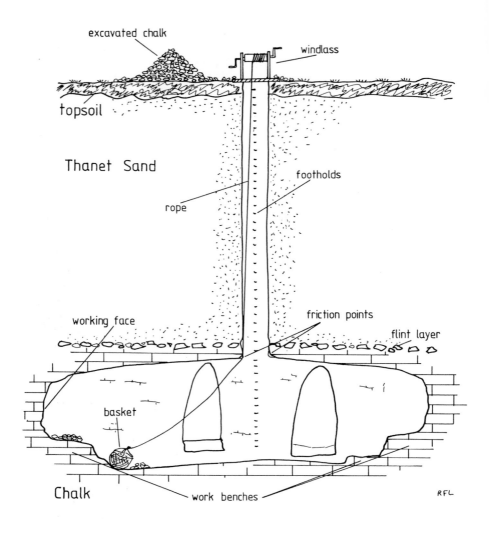

Fig.15 Deneholes — Method of Working

Denehole chamber showing jointing of chalk. (R. Le Gear)

Mining Methods — Chalkwells

Once again the shaft was sunk as close as possible to the field boundary, although some mining teams preferred to place the shaft in the centre of the field to be chalked. The chambers or 'wells' (usually three) were cut radially from the shaft. As the shaft was wider than the earlier types of denehole, the miner could not climb down and so was lowered on a rope by his colleagues. In some chalkwells, the shaft diameter increased as it went down so that rope friction was less of a problem and artificial light was not always necessary. In some examples, the length of the chambers are such that the chalk must have been transported to the base of the shaft by wheelbarrow. When enough chalk had been removed the chalkwell was sealed, usually by installing

Denehole chamber at bottom of shaft. (R. Le Gear)

a brick dome about 6ft down the shaft and backfilling to surface. When the brickwork fails, the shaft will open up.

From early writers we know that in the 17th century a mining team of three men would charge £10 to dig a chalkwell large enough to chalk a field of 6 acres. It would yield 360 tons of chalk i.e. a dressing of 60 tons per acre. If more than 6 acres needed treatment, the miners insisted on digging another shaft — for another £10 of course! A number of chalk-wells were dug by local farm labour when work was slack and these tend to be rougher and less stable than those dug by professionals. For those wishing to inspect a typical chalkwell in safety, a visit to Kent County Nurseries at Challock (TR003504) will be of interest. The 'Exotic Grotto' there is in actual fact a three-chambered chalkwell with a spiral staircase down the shaft. If you ignore the claims of it being a neolithic flint mine (as well as the gnomes and plants inside!) you will be able to see how it was excavated.

Groups of Deneholes

Although most deneholes are found singly and in distinct association with ancient field boundaries, some are found in groups of up to 70+ separate shafts. Great care was taken by the miners in these groups that individual deneholes did not communicate underground. Sometimes less than 3ft of chalk would separate two deneholes and this was to ensure the overall stability of the area and reduce the risk of subsidence.

The late John Caiger — pioneer of denehole research in the 1950s.   (N. Caiger)

John Caiger excavating floor of a denehole
chamber.   (N. Caiger)

Two of the largest groups are near Bexley, with 35+ at Cavey Springs
(TQ500727) and 50+ at Stankey Wood (TQ506728). Since it would be
both impractical and uneconomic to transport excavated chalk for any
distance, a denehole was dug as close as possible to the field it served.
The amount of chalk brought out of the denehole groups, however, far
exceeds that required for top dressing, even if the group had been
worked over long periods. It is therefore probable that the chalk was
used for other purposes as well. The deneholes of Cavey Springs, for
example, almost certainly supplied chalk blocks for building purposes.
Archaeological excavations and observations in Bexley village have
shown that several medieval buildings had footings of chalk blocks. No
doubt the chalk was also used on the local fields and some could have
been burnt in simple lime kilns in the vicinity of the mines.

The Development of the Denehole

The simplest, and almost certainly the earliest, type of denehole consisted of a very shallow bottle-shaped chamber, no more than 30ft deep.
F.C.J. Spurrell investigated a small number of these at Crayford in the

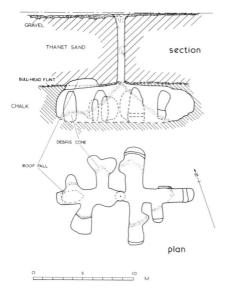

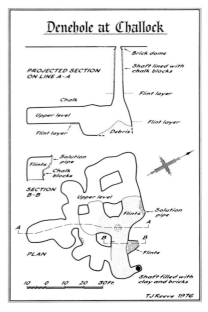

Fig.16 Denehole — Stankey Wood, Bexley

Fig.17 Denehole at Challock

late 19th century and he considered that they had been dug with deer antler picks. He had the mound of debris below the shaft carefully removed and found 'worked flints' and some Roman pottery. It is now realised, however, that you cannot conclusively date a denehole from what has fallen down the shaft. If the shaft had been dug through an earlier site, for instance, artifacts could fall out of the shaft sides at any time and give false evidence. In addition, pottery, etc. lying in surface soil can be washed into an open shaft after it has been abandoned. The unreliability of this method of dating was proved by R. Le Gear in 1964 whilst directing an excavation in a denehole near Dartford. A small fragment of Roman pottery was found but further down (indicating an earlier date) was a Victorian chamber pot! The pottery had in fact been washed into the shaft from a site further uphill.

The simple single-chambered denehole developed into a shaft with three short chambers radiating from the bottom. From this evolved the most prolific type found in North West Kent i.e. the double trefoil with two sets of three chambers on either side of the shaft (Figs. 16 and 17). This was an extremely good design combining efficient one man underground operations with structural stability. The mines of Stankey Wood in Bexley took the double trefoil one stage further by cutting away the sections of chalk separating the chambers, leaving up to six pillars to support the roof. This decreased the safety margin but increased output by up to 50%. Denehole excavation peaked around the 13th – 14th centuries when large areas of virgin woodland were being grubbed out and brought into agricultural use to satisfy the demands of an increasing population. Much of the woodland chosen was on a subsoil known as Thanet Sand which is slightly acidic or 'sour' and an application of chalk from deneholes was required to 'sweeten' it and thus improve productivity.

During the 15th – 16th centuries, the skill of sinking deneholes was apparently lost. One reason for this is believed to be the result of a sharp decrease in population (up to a third in some areas) following the outbreak of the Black Death. This hit England in 1349, with reoccurrences in 1362 and 1369, and from then on bad outbreaks occurred almost every decade. Another reason could be the introduction of sheep to the area at this time, with many fields turned over to grazing rather than crops. This decrease in agricultural demand meant that the skills of the denehole miner were no longer required, since there was now a surplus of cleared land.

By the 17th century, however, the population was once more on the increase and there was a demand for more woodland to be cleared for cultivation. It was now the turn of woodland on heavy clay soil to be cut down and chalk was required to break up the clay and assist drainage. Once again, shafts were sunk and chalk spread onto the fields. Now, however, the carefully efficient mining techniques of two centuries before had been lost and a new type of denehole was born, the chalk-well. The double trefoil pattern was no longer used and the excavations were much rougher in finish. This type continued to be dug right up to the turn of the present century. Possibly the last ever denehole to be dug in Kent was excavated near Doddington (TQ934573) by 'Tokey' Higgins between 1904 – 08. Fortunately, he was interviewed by a KURG member, Jim Bradshaw, shortly before his death in 1976 at the age of 92.

'. . . I had a small quarry and lime kell (kiln) just above the "Chequers" on Chequers Hill and, after an argument with the owner of the land, had to leave them. To stay in business, I moved up the hill on the same side and, on a small bit of ground, I built a brick kell and sank a draw well. This was in 1904 and at first I pulled up the chalk in baskets by hand with an old well-top windlass but later used an old horse that walked downhill and brought it up by block and tackle. I worked as a casual day labourer on the farms and lime burning was a "fall back" job. When the well was 20ft deep, I began to widen it as the old timers did until 1908 when I gave it up.'

This shaft has presumably now been filled since a bungalow has been built on the site. It must be stressed, in closing, that deneholes are dangerous places to explore since many are now in an unstable condition. In addition, hollows found in woods should be avoided since they could be denehole sites.

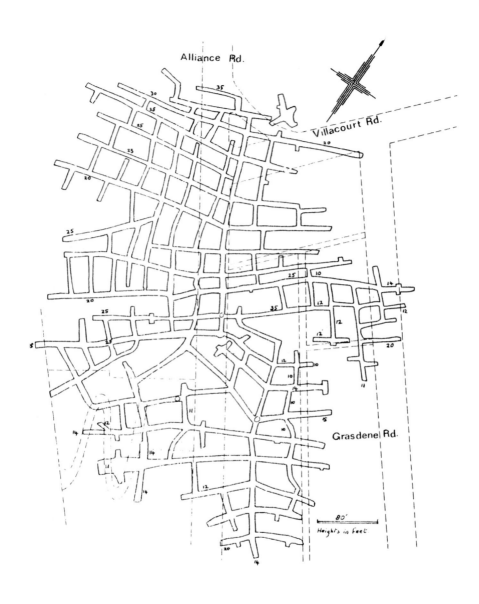

Fig.18 Plumstead Chalk Mine

Chalk Mines

Chalk is one of the most common rocks in Kent and Sussex but, to most people, the only known use has been where it was quarried to make cement. It has had other uses, however, for brickmaking, building and lime burning, and there were a number of quite extensive mines for this purpose. The dimensions of these mines were impressive, with passages up to 25ft high and a width of 15ft tapering to 6ft at the top. In cross-section they resembled a Norman arch and the practice of leaving solid pillars of chalk for support gave them the name of 'pillar and stall' mines. Since chalk is relatively soft, the passage ends were excavated by pick and shovel with the spoil being removed in baskets or wheelbarrows. Rather than excavate a 25ft high face, the technique was to drive a series of stepped 'benches' about 6ft high which allowed several men to work at the same time. The excavated chalk was thrown back onto the lower benches and so to the floor for collection. One departure from this method was to drive a face sloping at 45 degrees so that the chalk fell to the floor under its own weight. The chalk was stable enough to require no props but, if loose areas were encountered, the face was simply abandoned and carried on elsewhere. There was no problem from explosive gases and lighting was by candle or, at a later date, paraffin lamp.

Mines for Brickmaking

In the 19th century, Britain's economic expansion led to the creation of suburban London and an unprecedented demand for the supply of building materials to the capital. North-West Kent was admirably positioned to meet this demand and the Dover Road, the Medway and Thames Rivers and the expanding rail network provided an easy route for movement of materials. The area between Lewisham and Sittingbourne was subjected to massive opencast excavation of chalk for cement as well as clay for the yellow stock bricks which built most of Victorian London. A look at 19th century Ordnance Survey maps will show brickfields and clay pits in abundance and much of the area was lowered 6ft as the surface clay was stripped away.

There is no space to describe brickmaking operations in detail but several publications are included in the bibliography for those interested. The industry declined rapidly in the 1900s as clay deposits became depleted and cheaper bricks came on the market from around Fletton in Bedfordshire. Today there are only two working brickfields left and most of the others have been built upon. The yellow colour in the bricks came from adding about 15% chalk to the mixture and, although some brickfields had associated chalk quarries, many could not afford the space. The answer was to sink shafts on site and mine the chalk *in situ*. Some had inclined drift entrances to permit horse drawn trucks to enter the mine.

Plumstead Chalk Mines (Fig. 18)

These are situated at TQ463775 under Alliance Road, Grasdene Road, Villacourt Road and Sutherland Road. Between 1937 and 1950 the major topic of discussion for the inhabitants of the houses in these roads was the instability of the ground, which collapsed frequently in the roads, gardens and under houses! In September 1937 a collapse occurred at Rockcliffe Gardens in a children's playground, leaving a crater measuring 80ft x 60ft x 30ft deep. More collapses occurred in 1938 and Woolwich Borough Council employed consultants to carry out a series of bores to determine the extent of any cavities.

On 2nd June 1939, a party of Council workmen were filling in one of the boreholes. One of them, Samuel Gardner, was walking 10ft from the borehole when the ground suddenly subsided beneath him. At first, his head could be seen above the earth at the bottom of the crater but then the sides collapsed on him and he suffocated. The body was recovered from a depth of 30ft the following day. Collapses continued throughout the next decade but remedial action was prevented by the Second World War. The London County Council finally put through Parliament the LCC (Woolwich Subsidences) Act in 1950 and this empowered them to take whatever action was necessary to remedy the subsidences. Bores, headings and shafts were driven and surveys made, revealing the presence of a massive chalk mine. This was gradually filled by floating in pulverised fuel ash and, following this expensive operation, the ground stabilised.

The mines dated from the 19th century and were working up to 1920, being recorded by HM Inspector of Mines as South Metropolitan Mine, Gregory's Mine, King's Highway Mine and Cemetery Mine. They have also had other names at various times and may well be linked underground. We can get an idea of conditions from a report dated 1903:

'. . . Following the descent of the shaft on a hand-cranked winch . . . a lofty gallery runs through the dead white chalk to a working face 300 – 400 yards away, where the miners are busy with picks and shovels. Down the centre of the main galleries are two rows of flat metals on which run the small trolleys used to convey the chalk from the working face to the shaft. The mine manager himself superintends the driving of all new headings, shapes the roof and trims the corners; the workmen do the rough cutting after the roof has been secured. Throughout the mine the same bed of hard chalk forms a remarkably flat roof.'

Another report in 1906 says:
'. . . The brickyards, four in number, obtain chalk by shafts 120ft, 80ft and 150ft deep; the South Metropolitan Mine is entered by a sloping tunnel. Below Gregory's Brickyard, the aggregate length of the galleries is stated to be at least two miles. The tunnels are, as a rule, 9ft wide at floor level, diminishing to 3ft at the roof, and 25ft high; but these proportions are modified according to the harder or softer nature of the chalk, the presence of joints, etc. The mine was opened about 50 years ago.'

A further report in 1909 says:
'. . . the party, including the owner of the mine, became hopelessly lost while exploring the more remote disused galleries. Our guide was a man who had worked in the mine most of his life but we wandered in vain for over an hour, till reduced to our last candle, when, by a lucky mischance, one of the party, owing to the darkness, fell a distance of about 6ft. Happily he escaped without injury and discovered that he was in the newer workings and was able to direct us until an easier way out was found.'

Crayford Chalk Mines

These were similar in extent and old Ordnance Survey maps show a string of workings for clay and chalk between Erith and Crayford in the Slade Green area. The area was investigated by the archaeologist F.C.J. Spurrell at the turn of the century whilst looking for flint mines:
'. . . All of these caves formed part of a series . . . and one has been worked for chalk up to within the last 50 years, presenting a very interesting labyrinth of modern galleries, which have united several old shafts once separate. The great chalk pit was once a denehole in my recollection. The modern workings are for brickmaking purposes.'

The pit, now filled and overgrown, was at TQ518757. It was some 150ft in diameter and 49ft deep to the west of Maiden Lane. The 1862 Ordnance Survey map shows a rail track entering the pit and running up to what might have been a mine entrance at TQ517758. There was also an air shaft shown at TQ517757.

Dartford Chalk Mine (Fig. 19)

This is off Shepherds Lane at TQ531740 and the associated brickfield was owned by C.N. Kidd, who had several local businesses including a brewery. The brickfield itself is believed to date from 1886 and finally ceased just before the First World War. The older brickfield and the mine were to the north of the road and clay was excavated from an open pit to a depth of 13ft. This was connected to a smaller pit on the

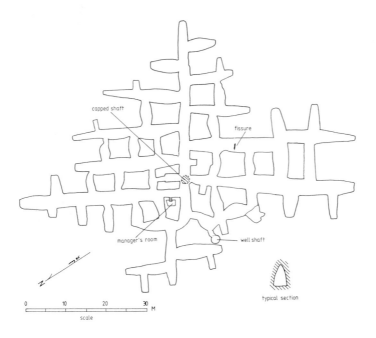

capped shaft

fissure

manager's room

well shaft

typical section

0 10 20 30 M

scale

R.F.L. 1988

Fig.19 Kidd's Chalk Mine, Shepherds Lane, Dartford

south side via a tunnel running under the road. Building development stopped expansion of the northern pit by 1890 and, although operations were transferred to the other one, it was decided to continue with the mine rather than sink a new one. Graffiti in the mine indicates that it ceased in 1911. The mine workings were underneath the eastern part of the pit and it was here that the crushing, etc. plant was situated. The washbacks (settling ponds) were wisely situated further away in view of the danger of leaks which could have flooded the mine. Perhaps this was a lesson learnt from the Cemetery Mine at Plumstead where such a leak caused a disastrous collapse.

There was a well near the mine shaft and, around 1920, a surface drain was diverted into it, a short tunnel being driven to connect it with the mine workings which acted as a soakaway. The original shaft was capped over about this time but it is not known why the drain wasn't diverted into this to save all the extra work! The area was used as a tip, mainly by Kidd's brewery for disposal of clinker and broken bottles, and the site of the shaft was lost under the fill.

Miners' graffiti in Dartford Chalk Mine 'Come unto me all ye that labour'.　　(A. Pearce)

The mine was re-entered in 1980 by members of Kent Underground Research Group, who used a wire ladder to gain access via the well. The workings were in good condition and there had been little change since the mine had ceased working. The 'tide marks' on the walls, however, showed that the drain had sometimes flooded the mine to a height of 5ft. There was a natural fissure in the floor which drained the water away but it obviously could not cope with sudden inflows. The galleries were on average 9ft wide at the base, tapering to 1ft 6in at roof level which was 20 – 30ft high.

The method of working in this mine was quite unusual. Instead of excavating the chalk in a series of benches up to 5ft high, here the benches were only a few inches high and less than 3ft deep. As the chalk from the face above fell down onto the floor, the benches broke up to leave a steep, slippery slope. This must have meant an awkward climb up to the face and difficult working conditions. A mine of this size rarely employed more than 2 – 3 men underground and it is likely that wheelbarrows were used to take the chalk to the shaft. Near the shaft is an interesting feature where a small room has been cut out with a flight of 4 steps up to it. This was probably a place where tools were stored and men had their meal breaks.

Dartford Chalk Mine. (R. Le Gear)

Descending well shaft entrance to Dartford Chalk Mine. (T. Reeve)

Dartford Chalk Mine. (R. Le Gear)

The shaft bottom was always a busy place in a mine and there are several deep rope grooves in the chalk where heavy loads were hauled up. A number of 'tally boards' were also cut into the walls to count the number of loads being taken out of a particular part of the mine. There are interesting graffiti here cut into the walls such as 'COME UNTO ME ALL THAT LABOUR', 'GOD IS LOVE' and the owner's name 'C.N. KIDD DARTFORD'. At one point in the mine, a miner's progress along a pilot side gallery can be traced from patches of soot on the roof. As he advanced the face 3ft or so, he moved his candle to a new position and there is a row of these patches leading back towards the main gallery. The candle holder was actually found still in place at the last position.

At some of the faces, miners had either carved their name on the walls or smoked it on the roof with a candle. Most of these were dated between 1901–1911 and a later one, 'A.E.J. Price 28.11.31', was probably a council official inspecting the drain. Even the mine engineman, R. Fulker, had found time to go down and leave his name carved for posterity. In 1988 the site was taken over to build houses and work was carried out to rock bolt and concrete some parts of the mine roof for stability. A ladder was installed in the well shaft and a manhole at the surface is situated in one of the access roads. Access is strictly controlled.

Frindsbury Chalk Mine

This was sited underneath Bill Street at TQ740702 and there was a shaft on either side of the road. It was commenced in the 19th century by the West family, who ran a large building and brickmaking business in the Medway Towns. Official figures give an annual output of around 400 tons of chalk and it is believed to have ceased around the late 1920s. Like many of this type of mine, it was operated on a shoestring budget and a traction engine pumped out the well and wound in the shaft using flat belts in the latter part of its life. There are no visible remains today, since the whole area has been built upon, but a number of subsidences have occurred. The history has already been published in some detail (see bibliography).

Mines for Building Material

Chalk is not a good building stone since it is very susceptible to erosion. It can, however, be used in house footings or road foundations since it is not so exposed to the atmosphere. Since the cost of purchasing and transporting chalk from nearby quarries could be prohibitive, there were occasions when it was mined *in situ*.

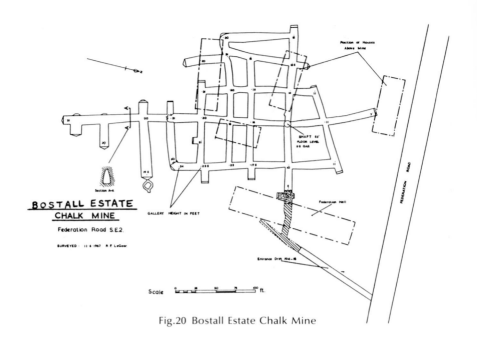

BOSTALL ESTATE
CHALK MINE

Federation Road S.E.2.

SURVEYED : 11 & 1967 R.F. LeGear

Scale

Fig.20 Bostall Estate Chalk Mine

Bostall Estate Chalk Mine (Fig. 20)

In 1899 the Royal Arsenal Co-operative Society embarked on an ambitious project — the building of an entire housing estate from scratch. The site chosen was at Abbey Wood (TQ471785) where they held land which had been used for market gardening. The RACS Works Dept moved from Woolwich to set up operations on the site with workshops and a light tramway to move materials around the area. To utilise local resources, a mine was excavated to provide chalk for the road foundations and lime for the internal plasterwork. Although it is generally referred to by the above name, it has also been known in the past as Suffolk Place Mine.

The 8ft diameter shaft was sunk in January 1900 to a depth of 60ft and headings were driven out to develop the mine. The floor was at the water table but this had been planned on purpose so that mortar could be mixed at surface with water pumped from the mine. The hard-worked engine which operated the pumps also drove the winding hoist in the shaft as well as machinery in the workshops via a system of shaft drives. By use of a dynamo it produced electric power and this mine was unique in being lit completely by electric light. The galleries average 10ft wide x 18ft high and the traditional method of benches was used to extract the chalk. The mine only had a short life and was abandoned in 1906, the building phase above ending eventually in 1914 after 1,052 houses had been built.

During the First World War, the mine was adapted as an air raid shelter and an inclined tunnel was driven down from surface. This subsequently suffered roof falls and, despite local protests, it was not reused again in 1939. It was next re-entered in 1967 by members of Kent Underground Research Group when an updated survey was carried out. The shaft was then resealed and access is restricted. The only thing remaining of the site today is the old works canteen which is now used by the council social services department.

Mines for Limeburning

The process of limeburning was carried out in kilns where chalk was burnt to produce quicklime (commonly called lime). When water was added to this, it became slaked lime which could be used for various purposes. As a fertiliser, it was much more efficient than spreading chalk alone since it could be absorbed into the soil straight away. In the building industry it was used to make plaster and, by adding sand, produced mortar. There were many small limekilns in Kent and Sussex and these were supplied from open pits or sometimes a denehole. When large quantities were required, however, it was not always practicable to excavate a quarry and sometimes associated chalk mines were excavated.

Chislehurst Chalk Mine (Fig. 21)

One of the largest of such mines was at Chislehurst and it is now open to the public as Chislehurst Caves (TQ433696). The chalk was first excavated and probably dates from medieval times. A document of that time refers to the 'Marlera at the Swellinde Pette in the Villa of Chislehurst' which has been translated as a marl pit in a hollow for burning chalk. A 17th century map refers to the woodland above the mine as Well Wood and this possibly refers to a denehole-type shaft for supplying chalk to the kilns.

The mine itself consists of three separate sets of galleries known as the Inner, Middle and Outer Series. The Outer Series was dug horizontally into the hill from the original chalk pit and is possibly the oldest of all, being less stable than the others and having suffered several roof falls in the past. It is the smallest mine and ceased operations before the galleries penetrated very far, probably around 1800.

The Inner Series was driven from a separate chalk pit to the South and an extensive set of galleries was worked from the East of the pit which contained the limekilns. In 1840 five kilns were being supplied from

CHISLEHURST CAVES

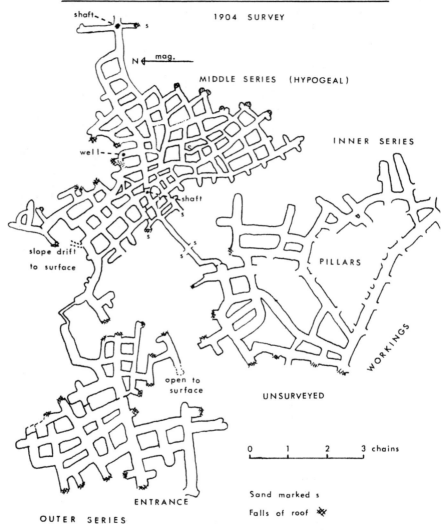

Fig.21 Chislehurst Caves

62

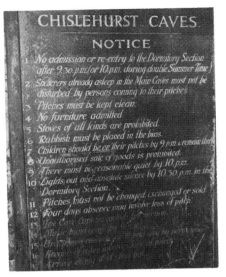

Chislehurst Caves (Chalk Mine).   (M. Jack)

Wartime notice at Chislehurst Caves when used as an air raid shelter.   (M. Jack)

these workings but severe flooding caused weakening of the galleries between 1855 and 1860 and several roof falls occurred.

The Middle Series dates from the same time, or perhaps slightly later, but was worked from an 85ft shaft further up the hill. The workings extended in all directions except to the South West because the mine manager knew of the proximity of the other two mines and of the property boundary at surface. Chalk was brought out of the shaft and either burnt at adjacent kilns or used in brickmaking. The will of James Taggart dated 1834 states: '. . . including the brickfields containing seven acres more or less and my freehold wood called Susan Wood, with lime kilns, brick kilns and chalk pit' (the word 'pit' in those days referred to a shaft).

Taggart left the business to his brother-in-law George Bascombe who continued to produce 'bricks, pots, lime and chalk' and intended to extend the mine workings further under the common to the North East. For this purpose, another shaft was sunk to avoid transporting the chalk a long way underground. Unlike the other two mines (which were driven horizontally and could use horse transport), wheelbarrows had to be used to transport the chalk to the shaft bottom. The ruts in the floor caused by these wheelbarrows were noted during an investigation of the workings in 1904. Despite the plans, the area around the second shaft was not fully developed and mining ceased around 1866. This was mainly due to the invention of the steam shovel because this machine could quickly remove large quantities of overburden. Large quarries were developed at Swanscombe, Northfleet and Gravesend which could produce chalk very cheaply. With the introduction of water transport and better roads, the local mines found it impossible to compete.

At some time prior to abandonment, two tunnels were driven to connect up with both the Outer and Inner Series which had already ceased. It seems likely that Bascombe wanted to check on the exact position of the other mines with a view to mining any unworked areas. Since Bascombe was a keen gardener, he adapted part of the Middle Series to grow celery and other vegetables and sunk a well in the mine to obtain water for the plants. A spiral passage was excavated into this section from his property on the surface and this is now known as 'Cavaliers Passage'. Bascombe was also a keen amateur archaeologist and it is perhaps significant that he did not consider any of the chalk workings to be ancient or mysterious.

In 1885, when mining had long since ceased, a great controversy arose as to the origins of the great chalk caverns. Almost as much correspondence was generated as in the argument about deneholes! At the turn of the century the owner of the Bickley Arms Hotel began to clear out parts of the mine and installed 'electric glowlamps'. He allowed members of the public to explore the mine and there was a visit in 1903 by a party of 'scientific men', including a Mr Nichols who was the Vice-President of the British Archaeological Association (the same organisation that Bascombe had belonged to!). Nichols published his opinions and concluded that the three sets of tunnels belonged to different periods, viz. Roman, Saxon and Druid. He dated Bascombe's well to the Roman period, called the stepped benches Druids' altars and interpreted the two haulage shafts as ancient deneholes of Celtic origin!

A further visit to the mine in 1904 included two mining engineers called T.E. and R.H. Forster. They stated that the caves were simply three chalk mines whose main excavations had been made in the 17th – 18th centuries. From then on, everyone joined in the argument with correspondence in the newspapers and heated debates at meetings. The advocates of the 'Druids theory' shouted down the chalk mine theorists and vice versa.

In the First World War the mines were used by the Government to store explosives and a light tramway was installed. It is said that the picric acid from the explosives turned the chalk yellow in some places. The wooden hut which is now the office dates from this time. In 1920

Eastry Chalk Mine. (M. Jack) Pratts Bottom Chalk Mine. (M. Jack)

the present owner acquired the site and attempted to grow mushrooms. During the Second World War the mines became the largest air raid shelter in the Greater London area with up to 8,000 people using it in 1940 at 1d per night. A new ventilation shaft was sunk together with powerful fans to keep the air flow circulating. New tunnels were driven to the surface to act as exits and a great deal of brickwork installed for toilets, washrooms, canteens and a first aid post. It was the wartime nurses, in fact, who drew the plan of the mines on the wall in the 'map room', through which visitors pass today.

Since the war, the mines have been open to the public as a show cave and the guides seem to have adopted Mr Nichols' version of the history as being more entertaining. Visitors are now shown Romans digging out chalk, Druids' sacrificial altars, a witch's cave and many other delights, including a ghost or two! Modern researchers, however, are convinced that the Victorian mining engineers were nearer the truth and that the main development of the mines took place in the late 18th to early 19th centuries. There were also similar chalk mines in the vicinity at Logs Hill and Camden Park.

Eastry Chalk Mine

A limeburning business was carried on by the Foord family at Eastry (TR309550) from 1811–1914 and a chalk mine was developed on several levels. The workings resemble a three dimensional maze and demonstrate the effect of mining without any forward planning. Access was originally by shaft but an inclined tunnel was later driven to the surface to emerge by the limekiln. The mine was abandoned following pressure from villagers who were worried that their houses were being undermined. It was subsequently turned into a folly and village festivities were held underground. It was the practice during these events to nail patterns of branches to the wall and the old nails still remain to puzzle visitors.

During the Second World War the long gallery was used by the Home Guard as a rifle range and the workings were later opened to the public as a show cave for a short time. It was during this period that two elaborate paintings resembling stained glass windows were placed on the walls. The mine is now on private property and access is strictly controlled but the owners have preserved the workings.

Attack & Defence

Until the development of large, long range cannons, military and civil defence activity was mostly carried out on the surface. Combat took place in the open, wherever armies happened to find themselves in proximity, and took the form of skirmishes, charges and close quarter fighting. Towns were fortified with keeps, moats and ramparts where the beseiged people spent most of the time awaiting relief from the rigours of isolation and starvation. Underground excavation was limited to dungeons, crypts and cellars, with the occasional sally port for a surprise attack or escape. The attackers occasionally attempted to undermine walls and battlements. Little of this underground activity has left any trace today.

The development of the large cannon, which could batter walls and armies from afar with impunity, must have seemed at first the ultimate weapon. The effect, however, was to send the whole concept of defence below ground, from which it has not emerged since. The design of fortifications underwent radical change with the disappearance of keeps and ramparts, development concentrating on the moat. A substantial ditch was dug up to 60ft deep and 100ft across, which could not be readily filled or bridged. Excavated material was used to build up an inner mound and the lines of approach were levelled to provide a clear arc of fire. The walls of the moat were lined with bricks or masonry, many feet thick, and a network of tunnels installed to enable men to move quickly around the fortification. Firing slits were positioned to create maximum havoc upon the enemy, gun batteries were built and, wherever possible, natural obstacles such as cliffs or hills were incorporated.

Thus protected, an army could sit out a siege, dominate communications and harry the enemy. This remained the situation until 1940 when the fortress at Eben Email fell to a new ultimate weapon — attack from the air. The Kent coast has many such fortifications and they are largely ignored in guide books in favour of more visually appealing surface structures. They are, nevertheless, equally impressive in terms of the ingenuity of their construction and their place in military history, even though none were put to the ultimate military test.

Western Heights, Dover

Although Dover Castle dominates the town, on the other side of the valley there is a discreet but no less impressive set of fortifications known as the Western Heights. The construction work started in 1779 to counter invasion threats from the French and Dutch, work gathering

Western Heights at Dover — Grand Shaft.
(M. Jack)

Western Heights at Dover — dry moat system.   (M. Jack)

momentum until 1814 when an armistice was signed. William Cobbett passed this way in 1823 on his 'Rural Rides' and commented '. . . a couple of square miles or so were hollowed out like a honeycomb, that either madness the most humiliating, or profligacy the most scandalous, must have been at work here for years'.

Despite such views, work soon began again with the threat of Napoleon III and the re-unification of Germany. The major works took place in 1850 and cost £300,000, which included removing the top of the hill and digging four miles of moats up to 60ft deep. The features are a maze of tunnels, cantilevered drawbridges, stairs, wells and firing positions. Although the features were connected by a continuous moat, they formed self-contained units which were capable of fighting on if part of the complex was overrun. The features are the Western Outworks (TR305404), Citadel (TR307404), Outer Bastion (TR307406), North Centre Bastion (TR313408) and Drop Redoubt (TR315412). The last two are now bisected by a road, for which the ditch has been filled in.

Another interesting feature is the Grand Shaft (TR316409) which was built in 1802 and connects the fortress with an entrance at the base of the cliff off Snargate Street. At the top, 59 steps lead down into a funnel-shaped depression where the 20ft wide shaft descends for 100ft. It is brick lined and there are three interlocking but separate spiral staircases, lit by apertures into the shaft. At the bottom, they all converge to join a passage out to the street. It is said that one staircase was for officers and ladies, another for women and the other for soldiers. Obviously Victorian morals decreed that the three types should never meet up on dark stairways! The sites can sometimes be visited by arrangement with Dover Council but the Citadel cannot, being occupied by a Borstal Institution.

The Medway Forts

Following a Dutch raid in 1667, a ring of forts was built around the town to protect the naval dockyard and these were improved and added to during the Napoleonic Wars. Despite the enormous cost, they never saw a shot fired in anger and Chatham today is still dominated by the largest, called Fort Amherst. Of the others, several have been demolished but some still remain, albeit hidden amongst trees or houses. These forts were smaller versions of the Dover fortifications and, although they had underground features, the local rumours of linking tunnels are not true. Fort Bridgewoods (TQ738652), Fort Clarence (TQ738674), Fort Delce (TQ746678), Fort Pitt (TQ751676) and Fort Darland (TQ782666) have been demolished although a few features may still be found.

Western Heights at Dover — North Centre Bastion. (M. Jack)

Western Heights at Dover — underground passage. (M. Jack)

Fort Borstal (TQ733664), Fort Horsted (TQ751650), Fort Luton (TQ762660), Twydall Redoubt (TQ795680) and Grange Redoubt (TQ797684) still remain at the time of writing but permission must be obtained from the respective landowners before visits. The most impressive was Fort Amherst (TQ759683) and, luckily for posterity, this has been preserved. It is open to the public and volunteers often dress up in period military uniform.

World War I
This marked a change in the pattern of warfare since the fighting took place in the trenches of France and Belgium, with no requirement for new fortifications in Britain. It did bring in a new development, however, whereby men of the Royal Engineers began to tunnel under the enemy trenches to lay explosive charges, hence the derivation of the word 'mine'. The base depot of the Royal Engineers was at Chatham and the area was used to experiment with new techniques of mining, since the local sand and chalk was almost identical to conditions at the Front. Very few of these trial mines were recorded at the time and, although it is likely that many collapsed subsequently, some still turn up in surprising places. The latest example was discovered following a collapse in a Gillingham back garden (TQ778689) in 1988.

During the construction of a roundabout at the junction of the A2 and A278 in Gillingham (TQ796664), a set of 6 galleries was found which had been unsuspected. They were found to be on three levels from 20 – 50ft below the surface, being dug as a model for mining operations under Hill 60 in France and the subsequent battle at Messines. Each gallery consisted of an entrance tunnel which led to six chambers, each 20ft wide x 30ft long x 7ft high. They were in a very dilapidated condition and had to be completely infilled.

World War II and After
The threat of air attack made it vital for the military to site important installations underground and this was especially so in the South East. Bunkers were excavated for radar stations at places such as St Margaret's Bay in Kent (TR361437) and Beachy Head in Sussex (TV580950). A headquarters bunker was sited at a place called the Wilderness near Tunbridge Wells (TQ574374) and a multi-level one underneath Dover Castle (TR325418). Home Guard posts were sited underground at a number of places in 1940 and, when invasion seemed imminent, similar sites were constructed for small commando units. The latter were supposed to come out after the enemy had passed by and to engage in guerilla warfare. One site still exists near Hollingbourne (TQ864556) but is well hidden. It is highly likely that

other undisclosed military installations exist in Kent and Sussex which are still regarded as military secrets.

Civilians also needed air raid shelters and large communal ones were made by adapting existing tunnel systems at Chatham, Rochester, Sevenoaks and Chislehurst. Perhaps the largest shelter in Britain was built in 1939 at Ramsgate (TR365642), part of which adapted the existing tunnel of a scenic railway. The system was 4 miles long and encircled the whole town, with several entrances to allow the citizens to shelter quickly when the sirens sounded. The tunnels were divided into sections with dormitory facilities, each allocated to a specific street. There was electric light from the town supply and hurricane lamps as a back up. The only things forbidden were smoking, pets and perambulators. The system is still intact but was sealed up after the war, access being closely controlled by the local council. At the time of writing there is talk of opening it up again as a museum.

Tunnels and Secret Passages

Whilst other parts of Britain have their tales of secret passages, for sheer numbers they are easily surpassed by the old smuggling counties of Kent and Sussex. Unfortunately for the romantics amongst us, the truth is that most of these sites have much humbler origins as drainage tunnels, cellars, follies, etc. Smugglers were practical men and it was far easier to carry goods at night on packhorses rather than drag them for long distances along wet, low passages. There is no denying that some passages were excavated for carrying and storing smuggled goods but a little thought will soon discount most of the rumours. Just about every church and large house has its accompanying secret passage rumour but nobody seems to know where it is! Take any two unexplained holes and someone will link them with a secret passage, be it 100 yards or 40 miles. For the dedicated hunter of secret passages, a host of rumours can be found in the publications of Chelsea Speleological Society (see bibliography) but a few examples are included below.

Smugglers' Passages

The Smugglers' Farm Hotel near Herstmonceux, Sussex (TQ667113) is a converted farmhouse dating from around 1600. In the Coffee Room is a primitive winch sited over a shallow shaft which is blocked at the bottom. The shaft is reputed to have led to a passage which came out on Pevensey Marshes and which was used by smugglers to bring their goods to a safe haven.

In the cliffs at Pegwell Bay, Kent (TR357644) there is a small opening about 8ft above the level of the beach. This leads to 500ft of low, artificial tunnel which passes under one shaft and is blocked at a second. It is called Frank Illingworth's Tunnel after the man who explored and wrote about it in 1938, his opinion being that it was driven by smugglers. At that time, it apparently went much further than today and Illingworth found an ancient pistol and 3 buttons from an Exciseman's tunic. The tunnel slopes slightly towards the beach and, since the cliff is continuously being eroded away, it is possible that it emerged at beach level when in use. The shaft is next to a demolished house and it is possible that smuggled goods were taken along the tunnel from the beach and up the shaft.

Secret Passages

A passage exists at Roedean School, Sussex (TQ348030) which connects the school with the beach. It was built in 1910 through chalk and is 3ft wide x 6ft high, being electrically lit throughout. A chamber has been

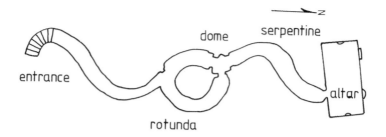

Fig.22 Margate Grotto

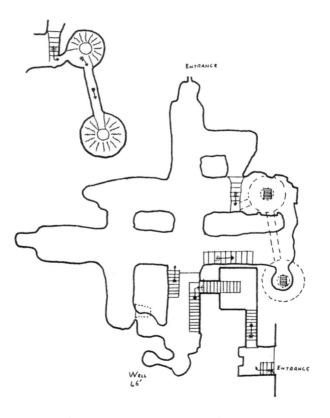

Fig.23 Vortigen's Cavern

excavated at the beach end as a changing room. The Roebuck Hotel at Wych Cross, Sussex (TQ420320) is said to have a concealed staircase behind the fireplace in the bar. This leads down to cellars and out to Dane Hill via a passage.

Follies

Margate in Kent has more than its share of strange underground places. It is not known when the Margate Grotto (TR362708) was excavated but it was re-discovered in 1835 when a workman dug through the cover of what he thought was a well. The landowner, Mr Newlove, was too portly to enter the hole but his son was lowered 20ft to the floor of a tunnel. To his amazement, he found himself wandering around a sensationally decorated grotto where the walls were decorated with sea shells in all types of pattern (Fig. 22).

The Grotto is open to the public and modern visitors enter via a specially constructed entrance. The shapes of flowers, hearts and trees abound right up to the end, some 104ft from the entrance. In the absence of scientific dating, the grotto has been subject to much fanciful speculation which has linked it to the Trojans and Phoenicians. It is much more recent than that but still worth a visit.

Nearby in Cliftonville is King Vortigern's Cavern which is also open to the public. Like the Grotto, it was re-discovered accidentally in 1798 but the paintings were added subsequently by successive owners. The star attraction is a life size painting of the King which fluoresces under ultra violet light. The tunnels are on more than one level (Fig. 23) and there are two curious circular chambers. The guides would have us believe that the latter were for holding prisoners but they are more likely to have been Ice Wells.

In the grounds of Kent County Nurseries at Challock (TR003504) lies what is termed the Challock Exotic Grotto. It is claimed to be a Neolithic flint mine and there is a spiral staircase descending the 30ft shaft, at the base of which three large chambers have been decked out with plants, statues and waterfalls. It is in reality a chalkwell, perhaps 200 years old, but it is well preserved and worth a visit to see how they were excavated (if you can ignore the shrubbery!).

Crypts

The crypt of Hythe Church (TR161349) is not strictly speaking below ground but for those with a macabre interest it is worth a visit as it contains an ossuary. Some 1,100 skulls and 8,000 thigh bones, thought to be a relic of the Black Death, have been arranged around the walls in gruesome decorative piles. The original date of the church is 1100 AD so some of these bones may be of considerable antiquity.

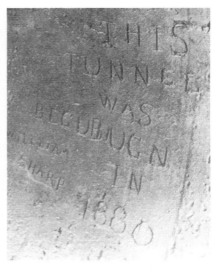

Frank Illingworth's Tunnel — passage near shaft. (T. Reeve)

Inscription in old Channel Tunnel. 'This tunnel was begun in 1880 — William Sharp' (M. Jack)

Frank Illingworth's Tunnel — entrance above figure. (T. Reeve)

Conduits

Greenwich Park in London (TQ392773) has plenty of underground phenomena but there are a number of unique conduits which were dug in the sub-surface gravel to collect water for a nearby Royal Palace. They average 5ft high x 2ft 6ins wide and are brick-lined with an arched roof. Gaps were left in the bottom three courses of bricks to allow water to percolate through and this was channelled along a lead-lined trough in the floor. Some conduits are long, single passages, up to a quarter of a mile long, with occasional manholes to the surface. Others have many branches but they are all fulfilling their original purpose; where the water goes to now is something of a mystery. Access is strictly restricted by the park authorities.

Another use for conduits was to take water away from buildings. The large roof area of Canterbury Cathedral (TR151579) collected a great volume of rainwater and this is directed into a series of old underground conduits. Like at Greenwich, they are mostly brick-lined with an arched roof and have a number of access manholes.

Horizontal Wells

This seems to be an anomaly at first sight but tunnel systems have been driven into the chalk at a number of places to collect water. At Terlingham near Folkestone (TR211381), a reservoir is supplied by water issuing from such a tunnel. This consists of nearly 700 yards of passage and, at intervals of 8ft, holes have been drilled for 25ft up into the roof. These tap water bearing layers of rock above and the water pours down into the passage and out to the reservoir.

Channel Tunnel

At the time of writing, the new Channel Tunnel has not yet been finished but this attempt is only one of many in the past. Smaller versions exist at Abbotts Cliff near Folkestone (TR263384) and Shakespeare Cliff near Dover (TR295393). These were started in the 1880s by Sir Edward Watkin but the attempt was stopped following political pressure over fear of invasion. By walking along the seafront from Folkestone towards Dover, a series of short gated tunnels are passed on the left which drain the bed of the railway track above. One of these intersects the old Channel Tunnel which is accessible for over 500ft until it becomes flooded. It was only driven for a short distance but it was one of the first instances of using a tunnelling machine and this has left a circular cross-section, 7ft in diameter. Nearby is the site of a further attempt in 1922 which used a boring machine designed to tunnel under the German lines in the First World War. This only went for 400ft before the machine broke down and the latter can be seen

Old Channel Tunnel — bored passage. (M. Jack)

Remains of old Channel Tunnel boring machine. (M. Jack)

sticking out of the hillside where it was abandoned. It was quite a monster machine for its day and drove a 12ft diameter circular tunnel at 12ft per hour.

Miscellaneous

Situated beneath The Point at Blackheath, London, is the site of Blackheath Cavern. This was originally a chalk mine but in the late 18th century it achieved a certain fame, verging on notoriety. In 1780 it was a fashionable curiosity, entered by paying 6d at Caves Cottage and descending 40 steps to see two caverns and a well 21ft deep. A young woman is reputed to have entered the cavern and '. . . fell in a fit and expired in about half an hour'. It later became known as Jack Cade's Cavern and became the venue for drinking parties complete with chandelier and bar. Following complaints, it was sealed off in 1854 and, although it was reopened in 1939, it was later resealed.

At the Royal Observatory in Greenwich Park, the Astronomer Royal called Flamsteed constructed a 100ft vertical shaft in 1670. This was descended by spiral staircase and observations of the sky could take place at the bottom. The building is now a museum and visitors can still view the well.

A Mystery

It seems worth ending with a mystery to show the reader that there is plenty of other subterranean activity in the region that awaits examination and explanation. In 1968, Neil Young of Chelsea Speleological Society examined a hole at Tenterden (TQ917318) following press reports. He found a shaft over 30ft deep but could not enter due to its narrowness at the top. The intriguing feature was that it gave out a loud roaring sound. By lowering a microphone and testing with a handkerchief, he found that the sound was caused by air being sucked continuously into the hole and being compressed as it passed the constriction. By using a mirror and spotlight, he established that there was a water surface at the base of the shaft.

The site remains a mystery. There is no record of any drain or underground watercourse in the vicinity but the most reasonable explanation was that the passage of water was drawing in the air and that there must be a substantial cavity to absorb it. Is it natural? Is it man-made? Nobody has found out.

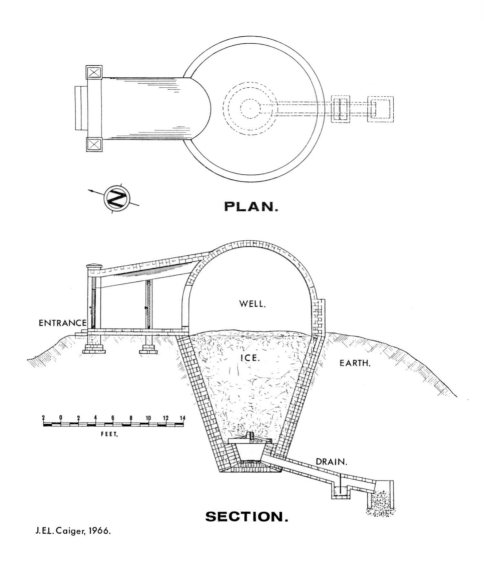

PLAN.

ENTRANCE

WELL.

ICE.

EARTH.

2 0 2 4 6 8 10 12 14
FEET.

DRAIN.

SECTION.

J.E.L.Caiger, 1966.

Fig.24 An Ice-Well at Frognal, Chislehurst

Underground Domestic Facilities

The old saying 'there is nothing new under the sun' is very apt when comparing the contents of a modern kitchen with those of earlier times. All facilities were there, albeit in a more primitive form. On large estates in the 18th and early 19th centuries, the domestic offices were situated away from the main building complex. The former were extensive with brew houses and fuel sheds above ground but a number of places were sited underground, e.g. meat stores, vegetable cellars, ice wells, water cisterns, etc. All were essential to the smooth running of an estate which often catered for large numbers of workers as well as the residents.

If the gardens had been landscaped by an expert, they sometimes included a bath house, dairy, grottos, ornamental ponds and lakes — all requiring a complicated system of water supply and disposal. Channels and drains were laid and settling tanks, storage cisterns and pumps installed. Two of the most common utilitarian out-buildings still surviving today are the Ice Well and Cesspit, often in surprisingly good condition after 200 years or longer. This may be due to the fact that in underground design the buildings were somewhat similar with deep brick-lined pits sunk into the ground, wide at the top and tapering towards the bottom. They were usually disguised to blend into the surroundings by the addition of a plant and tree covered mound or a summer house type of superstructure.

Ice Wells

These were devices for storing ice which was collected in winter from a nearby pond or lake. They were constructed either completely or partly underground and were lined with bricks as an egg-shaped or domed container (Figs. 24 & 25). In order to stop the ice from melting for as long as possible (this could be for many months or even up to a year) they were made with cavity walls for maximum insulation. Strong double doors, facing North, were fitted to the entrance passage. Naturally, some of the ice melted during the year and the accumulated melt-water was drained away at the base of the structure. A drain or soakaway was constructed in the floor for this purpose and was fitted with a vermin-proof barrier. The earth mound covering the dome was planted with shady trees and ivy, which was believed to keep the mound cool and dry through the process of evaporation.

An Ice House was a building above ground for storing ice and foodstuffs, often used to hang meat and game. In the past, this has often led to confusion since not all Ice Wells have 'houses' and not all Ice Houses

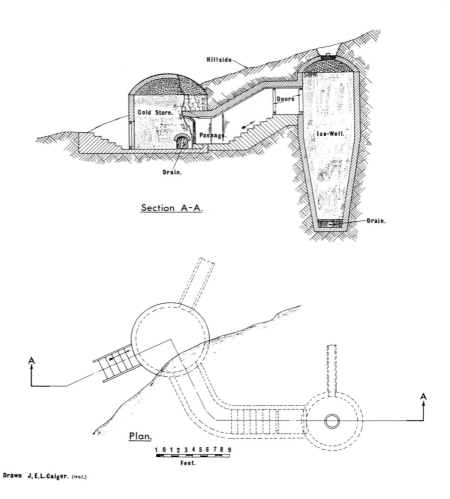

Section A-A.

Plan.

1 0 1 2 3 4 5 6 7 8 9
Feet.

Drawn J, E.L. Caiger. (1967.)

Fig.25 Ice-House in Royal Military Repository Grounds, Woolwich

have 'wells'. Landscape gardeners of the 18th and early 19th centuries differentiate quite clearly in their specifications for each structure, starting with the 'Ice Hole' which was little more than a brick-lined pit, insulated on all sides with a removable insulated top. This was comparatively cheap to build and maintain. Ice Wells and Houses were more elaborate and expensive, and many variations on the basic design still exist today. It is interesting to examine original drawings and plans designed by the leading landscape gardeners of the day, each one

Water conduit at Hythe. (M. Jack)

competing against the other to produce the most original and 'cunning' (unobtrusive or decorative) exterior to these somewhat mundane domestic buildings.

The use of ice for keeping food fresh is very ancient. The Romans certainly regarded it as a desirable asset to be able to serve cool drinks to guests, but the use of ice in Britain did not become common until the 17th century. It is believed that Ice Wells were introduced from France by King Charles II who had one built at Upper St James Park (now Green Park) in 1664. Ice was regarded as a super luxury and, during the 18th century, the possession of an Ice Well was something of a status symbol. It is unlikely that the ice itself was used in culinary or medicinal recipes, but pans of clean water were placed in the Ice Well to freeze over. This was then used to cool wine or in the kitchen to speed the setting of jellies, etc. and to keep meat fresh in hot weather. In the sick room it was used to cool fevers, an essential treatment in an age when a high temperature or bout of 'flu could kill. One drastic measure was to immerse a patient in a bath of water and crushed ice, a treatment known as a 'slush bath'.

Fig.26 Preparing an Ice-Well

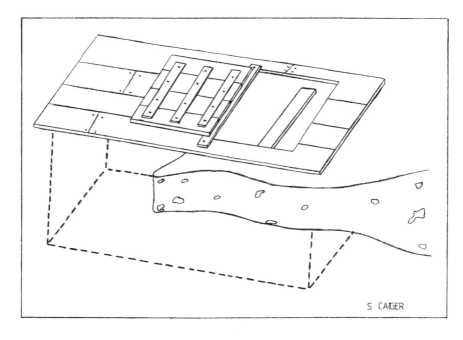

S CAIGER

Fig.27 Wooden Cover to a Mediaeval Cesspit

Access hole of filled-in cesspit at Frindsbury.   (A. Pearce)

Ice Well at Goodnestone — edge of
chamber.   (M. Jack)

Preparing the Ice Well (Fig. 26) was a complicated task, usually carried out under the supervision of the head gardener. In late autumn it was emptied of all previous residue and the interior was carefully cleaned and given a coat of lime wash. The doors and the trap door in the roof were left open to allow air to circulate and sacks of unslaked lime were placed inside to absorb any moisture. As soon as the pond froze over, all available hands were drafted in to fill the Ice Well as soon as possible. If the weather was not severe enough to freeze water into ice, compacted snow would be used instead.

The walls were lined with bundles of barley straw to improve insulation and to assist with drainage of the melt-water. Alternate layers of ice and straw were then placed in the well and rammed in to make a solid freezing mass. When full, the trap door in the roof was closed and sealed with clay to make it airtight. Entry to the well was restricted as much as possible and the system of double doors kept the cold air from escaping. The filling of Ice Wells was always a gamble and, if possible, ice would be collected after a particularly hard frost when it was regarded as being purer and more free from sediment.

By the beginning of the 19th century, natural ice from Norway was being shipped over and, with the advent of railways, transportation of

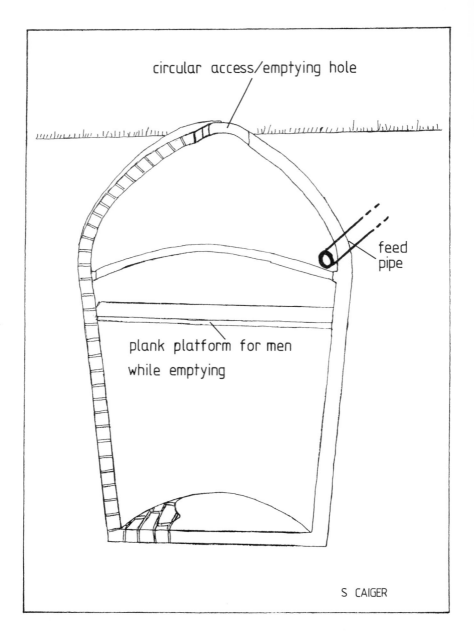

Fig.28 Typical Bricklined 19th Century Cesspit

ice became commonplace. Most households had an ice box sunk in a shady part of the garden and ice was being delivered in slabs by regular roundsmen. Ice Wells became obsolete, although there is a record of one being used as late as the 1920s. It is always a worthwhile effort when visiting a stately home to take a walk around the grounds. There are still a number of Ice Wells surviving and many are in excellent condition, such as those at Green Street Green (TQ5870) and Bromley (TQ411700).

Cesspits

There is no polite way to describe a lavatory; it is what it is and no dressing up with different names like 'loo' can alter the fact that its function is to dispose of human waste in as discreet and hygienic a manner as possible. A quick flush and as far as we are concerned it is out of sight and out of mind. Few people in Kent in this day and age would boast about owning a cesspit (or if they do it is referred to as a 'septic tank') but in country districts this is often still the only means of waste disposal available.

The cost and inconvenience of emptying a cesspit today is prohibitive and most people convert to mains drainage when the opportunity arrives. In early years, however, the cesspit was quite common and even some large Victorian villas, set in neat rows in the suburbs of London, had cesspits rather than drains to proper sewers. Very large numbers of these survive underground and are constantly being discovered by builders re-developing an old neighbourhood.

At Bexleyheath, during the clearing of a site now occupied by Woolwich Building Society offices, some 42 cesspits were uncovered during the demolition of a row of small Victorian and Edwardian houses. As these had been anticipated, they were dealt with promptly by the contractors as well as archaeologists, to whom the uncovering of a cesspit is an interesting find indeed. Many odd items of everyday life were washed into the unsavoury depths and, as the losers were invariably unwilling to risk retrieving them, we can gain interesting artifacts from such sources.

The siting of a cesspit was of great importance as seepage of pollutants into drinking water was a constant hazard. All too often the simple rules of hygiene were ignored by ordinary households and the dumping of sewage near water supplies undoubtedly contributed to the epidemics of plague, etc. which decimated many medieval villages. The Black Death forced people to change their habits and rules were introduced in towns forcing people to dig cesspits. These were emptied periodically by 'gongfermers' or 'night men' who were highly paid for this unpleasant duty. Some cesspits were so large that it took several nights to empty them and one under Newgate Gaol in 1281 took 13 men

5 nights to clear. In the early days the waste was taken outside the town boundaries and often sold to farmers as a fertiliser. Eventually, however, the amount became so great that it was emptied into the nearest river in the forlorn hope that it would be dispersed elsewhere. Even today, this practice is carried on by a number of water authorities.

The size and shape of cesspits has varied greatly down the years but most consist of a brick-lined pit with some form of cover (Fig. 28). Gaps were left in the brickwork at the sides and bottom to allow the liquid to drain away. Medieval ones tended to be large (Fig. 27) and some were associated with complex drainage systems. At Boxley Abbey, Kent, there is a good example of an associated drain which is large enough to stand up in. This connected with the 'Neccessarium' above and, by a system of sluices, water from a nearby stream could be directed into the drain to flush the waste into the cesspit. Many so-called secret passages are really humble sewerage systems!

Georgian cesspits were much smaller and, rather than empty them when full, it was often the practice to dig a new one. It is thus possible to find two or three cesspits side by side which span several decades of use. In Victorian times, the numerous terraced houses had to site the cesspits at the end of the garden and it was often the practice for several houses to share a common cesspit. Most such terraces have an alley along the back of the garden and this was to allow access for the 'night men'. Bad plumbing was common at that time and there were many music hall jokes about 'the drains', visitors being expected politely to ignore the smell.

A common practice in parts of Kent was to knock the bottom completely out of cesspits and this would allow more to drain away into the chalk. Although this meant that they didn't need to be emptied so often, it was rather short-sighted since wells took water from the same chalk! Water from the chalk of the Medway area is still high in nitrate content for this reason. Archaeological excavation of a cesspit is not everyone's choice but analysis of the soil content can yield interesting insights into the diets of people using it.

Many cesspits would have been filled in when abandoned but some were merely covered over with a slab or wooden cover. Examples open up from time to time but they are rarely deep enough to present a danger. In some places, however, houses adapted abandoned dene-holes as cesspits which were ideal since the underground space meant that they never needed emptying. The top part of the shaft was lined with bricks and arched over at the top, sometimes with a small access hole. Earthenware pipes directed the sewage into the shaft and this has caused problems in the past where the brick lining has been eroded and fallen away.

Water Cisterns

Another underground feature found in bigger houses was the water cistern. This was a large brick-lined chamber which was made watertight and arched over with a small access hole. Rain water from the roof was directed into the cistern where it could be stored for future use, being softer than water drawn from a well in the chalk. Sometimes a pipe connected the cistern to a hand pump in the kitchen. Like cesspits, a number of water cisterns were merely slabbed over when abandoned but the workmanship often means that the brickwork is still sound.

Medieval well exposed in cliff at Birling Gap, Sussex. (T. Reeve)

Well windlass at Cobbs Hall, Addington. (M. Jack)

Wells

Many of us are so used to merely turning on a tap nowadays that we cannot visualise what it was like before a mains water supply became available. As recently as 100 years ago, most people had to make their own arrangements to obtain water and this often meant taking it from the nearest river or stream. This had its dangers in that they never knew what had been placed in further upstream and disease was common. The use of a stream was not always possible, however, and the chalk areas of Kent and Sussex are usually completely devoid of surface water. The only answer was to dig down to find water and wells were essential in such places. The possession of a well was thus not only more convenient but also much safer, since the water had usually been filtered in passing through the surrounding rock. At one time, each village had its own communal well but, by the end of the 19th century, most houses had their own.

The depths of wells is governed by the level of the local water table, which is the highest point at which the rock is completely saturated with water. Near the coast, the water table will be at or near sea level but this rises further inland at a gradient of about 1 in 200. It is not as simple as this, however, since some layers of rock are impervious and the water draining down from surface cannot go any deeper once it has reached this point. The rock above this impervious layer thus becomes locally saturated and there is a 'perched' water table much higher than normal. Conversely, there are occasions when strata occurs at an angle and water bearing rock is overlain by an impervious layer. Surface water enters the lower layer some distance away and travels sideways to saturate the whole length of that layer. At a particular point, therefore, the 'normal' water table could be a great deal higher than it is but the water is prevented from rising to that point by an impervious layer above. Once the impervious layer is pierced, water is forced up under pressure and some low-lying wells actually have water flowing over the top! This is the principle behind artesian wells and the advantage is that the water does not have to be pumped out. As soon as a well has been sunk, water will seep in until the water reaches its natural level and this is called the 'Rest Water Level' (or RWL). In some areas towards the end of the 19th century, so much water was being extracted that the water table dropped and many wells had to be deepened when they ran dry. Nowadays, much of our water supply comes from surface reservoirs and the RWL of old wells has risen again as the water table returns to normal.

Wells have been dug for centuries and most were excavated by teams of professional well diggers. These were an itinerant breed of men who wandered the countryside and it is likely that they turned their hand to digging denehole shafts when work was slack. They were summed up by John Bannister in 1799:

'. . . These accidents render this profession extremely hazardous, but as the people who embark in it entertain but little thoughts of a future period, and since the chief end of their pursuits is the obtaining of a liberal supply of drink, if this end be answered they bestow little attention to the hazards of their profession . . . '

A well was started by marking off a circle on the ground, 18 inches greater in circumference than the intended dimension of the well. A wooden platform was then laid down with a hole cut out corresponding to the required diameter. A tripod was erected over the hole and a windlass placed to one side. Due to the restricted space in the well, the tools used by the digger all had small handles and the most commonly used were a mattock-like pick and a round faced shovel called a 'graft'. A wicker basket with two handles was used to remove the spoil and this was placed between the digger's legs whilst working. Two tallow candles were placed on either side of the shaft and this gave light without casting a shadow. The digger descended by sitting on a horizontal stick which was tied onto the bottom of the rope. This was quite comfortable and he could sit on this for some hours, especially when installing the well lining.

One of the first problems was to hold back the loose upper strata until solid rock was reached and, for this, a lining to the sides was necessary. This lining was called 'steining' and either bricks, stone blocks or flints were used. The local expression for bricking a well was 'steaming up' and the quality of the brickwork depended on how much the customer was prepared to pay. A good steining consisted of bricks laid lengthwise (stretchers) and sometimes these were doubled if the shaft was sunk through loose sand. Another method was to lay bricks end on (headers) and a course of headers was sometimes mixed with stretchers to give extra stability. In cheap wells, old reject half bricks (bats) were used and the ends were chipped to fit into the curve of the shaft. Since the soil behind would usually keep brickwork in place, steining was normally laid 'dry' except for the top 3ft which was mortared.

Two main methods of sinking were used. In the first, the well was sunk as far as it would go without falling in and then a circular 'curb' was laid at the bottom. The curb was made of sections of 4 inch thick wood, joined together, and the steining was built up on this to the surface with earth packed firmly behind it. A small pit was then dug in the centre of the floor and a platform of boards laid at the bottom. Notches were cut in the walls and lengths of timber called 'raking props' jammed in to support the curb above. The earth below was then excavated to the full diameter and another curb laid at the bottom, with steining installed up to the upper curb. The sections of the upper curb were then removed and steining inserted to make it continuous. This sequence was repeated until solid rock was reached, at which point a ledge was cut out for the whole steining to rest upon.

In the other method, a 'tun' was used which looked like a large barrel with half the staves removed. It was 6ft high, the diameter of the well without steining and the vertical boards were 1 inch thick was a spacing of 4–6 inches. The tun was lowered as the shaft was sunk and it gave protection to the digger working inside. When it reached a depth of 6ft, the tun formed a base on which the steining was built up to the surface. The digger then excavated underneath the tun, which sank at the same time under the weight of the steining. As soon as a further 6ft had been sunk, an extra section of steining was added to take it to the surface. In this way, the well was sunk until solid rock was reached and the steining followed the tun down the shaft, with more being added to the top as it progressed. A ledge was cut in the rock for the steining to rest upon and the tun removed. If solid rock was not reached, the tun was abandoned at the bottom of the well.

Once solid rock was reached, the sides no longer needed support but progress depended on how hard the rock was. Chalk was easily excavated by hand pick but some other types of rock needed explosive. Below about 40ft, bad air became a problem and this was especially so in chalk which produced carbon dioxide, a gas that is heavier than air. Various methods of ventilation were used, some quite bizarre but effective. Quick lime in a bucket was often lowered to the bottom at night and this usually absorbed bad air by the time work started in the morning. If not, a bale of hay was tied to the rope and thrown down the shaft a few times, thus forcing fresh air to the bottom. One local practice used a large upended umbrella which had the same effect! Before descending a shaft in the morning, the digger would test the air by lowering a candle in a bucket.

The usual method was to charge a certain price for sinking to solid rock and then agreeing a new price for each subsequent 20–25ft. This allowed the well diggers to take account of any unsuspected problems such as very hard rock or a layer of shifting sand. In the latter case, a special tun was made with bowed sides which were pulled in with an iron band. When placed in position, the band was removed and the sides automatically pushed outwards to jam the tun at that point. The decision on how deep to sink the well was fairly easy but very much 'rule of thumb'. The well was considered deep enough if, first thing in the morning, it took more than an hour to empty it by continuous bailing. Other diggers stopped when the water was thigh deep or they were excavating one part of water to two parts of spoil.

Sometimes the water was so deep that a borehole was sunk instead or even a well sunk so far and then continued as a borehole. The advantage of a borehole was that it was quicker and cheaper to sink but it could not be descended subsequently like a well if maintenance was needed. In clay and soft rock, a large auger was used which was manually turned at the surface. In harder rock, however, it was necessary to use a chisel bit attached to a rope which, by being alternately raised and dropped, would break up the rock. After a short period of boring, the chisel bit was removed and a shell-pump lowered. This was a cylinder with a hinged bottom opening upwards and, when dropped into the hole, would trap the debris which could be pulled up with the shell-pump.

Domestic Wells

These were from 3–4ft in diameter and normally covered with a wooden lid or slab, water being pulled up by a bucket on a rope. Some were more elaborate with low brick walls at the surface and a windlass operated by hand or horse. Most were sited in the back garden near the house and many old houses still have their wells, albeit covered over and forgotten. With the introduction of terraced housing, it became impracticable to have a well for each house and there was usually a communal one for several houses, reached from the alley to the rear. When old houses are demolished for re-development, the old wells are often forgotten about and there have been a number of subsequent subsidences when the well cover has given way.

A domestic well was recently discovered under the floor of Yokes Court near Frinsted (TQ899565) and this was pumped out and explored by members of Kent Underground Research Group. It was over 300ft deep but rubble had been thrown in at some time in the past and the original bottom was not reached. An interesting feature was that footholds had been cut into the sides of the well to a depth of 200ft, presumably when it was being sunk. In the room above, one of the exposed beams had a notch cut out where a pulley wheel had obviously assisted in pulling up the buckets of water. A more interesting haulage device was used at a well at St Radigund's Abbey near Dover (TR275419). This dates from the 12th century and there is a special well house with a wooden 'horse gin'. The latter consists of a vertical windlass with a horizontal beam that was pulled round by a horse. Although the well is reputed to be 450ft deep, the RWL was only 183ft in 1966. The horse gin is still *in situ*.

Agricultural Wells

As the name suggests, these supplied water for farm animals or orchards where there was no surface source. Stables of large estates often had their own well, as did remote barns where cattle were kept away from the main farm. Most growing crops had to rely on natural rainfall but where lack of water could be a disaster, such as remote orchards, a well was sunk as an emergency source. These wells were similar in structure to the domestic type and were usually covered with a slab. Examples of such remote wells are near Hucking in Kent (TQ842584) and Canadia in Sussex (TQ742182). Sometimes wells occur in remote woods and it can be puzzling why they were ever placed there. These are usually the only visible remains of very old settlements which have since become disused and overgrown.

Industrial Wells

A number of large factories in the 19th century often needed a great volume of water and thus sank their own wells, with pumps to ensure a continuing flow. Since the extraction rate was much greater than a domestic well, they had to go deeper to ensure a continuing supply and often used boreholes. Where a traditional well was sunk, these were much wider and anything up to 10ft in diameter. Certain industrial processes needed soft water but there could be problems with ordinary wells, e.g. those near the coast could have brackish water and those in chalk gave hard water. The answer in this case was to sink right through the chalk to reach the Lower Greensand Beds which gave a supply of soft water, sealing off the well from the chalk layer to prevent intermixing. All disused brickfields and cement works would have had their own wells but these were often merely covered over when abandoned. An example of a brickfield well (with a 12-inch bore) is at Newgardens in Kent (TQ950629) where the pumping apparatus was still in place at the time of writing.

With the introduction of mains water supply, wells did not become completely obsolete. Many Water Boards in areas on the chalk sank large wells to obtain the water that they treated and distributed. To increase the flow still further, horizontal passages were driven from the sides of the well for hundreds of feet so that a bigger area could be tapped. These systems are almost underground reservoirs and many are still used or kept as emergency supplies. A typical example is the Luton Pumping Station at Chatham (TQ775663) where 10 separate wells have been sunk to 150ft and all are interconnected by headings to form one system. There is a total of over 5,000ft of these headings which average 9ft x 7ft in cross-section. The Ramsgate water supply is even larger with over 5 miles of horizontal passages. Some water authorities even drove horizontal wells into the chalk which consisted of branched adits with boreholes in the roof.

Sea cave at Botany Bay, Kent. (T. Reeve)

Sea cave at Birling Gap, Sussex. (T. Reeve)

Natural Caves

Although the geology of Kent and Sussex is not particularly good for the formation of natural caves, a number of recent discoveries have shown that, contrary to the opinion of many cavers and geologists, quite extensive cave systems can be found in the chalk. Small caves also occur in other rocks, including sandstone and 'Kentish Rag' (a sandy limestone), and include several important sites of archaeological or palaeontological interest. There are also numerous examples of sea-worn caves scattered around the chalk cliffs of the Kent and Sussex coastline. None of the latter are very extensive, only rarely going beyond the limit of daylight penetration, but they can be quite roomy and make nonsense of the widely-held belief that chalk is too unstable for cave development. One example in the Seven Sisters cliff near Cuckmere (TV5396) measures 65ft in length and up to 50ft wide.

The processes involved in the formation of inland caves in chalk or limestone are extremely complex and are still not fully understood. Basically they are the result of water dissolving and eroding the rock along crevices known as joints, bedding planes and faults. Caves formed by free flowing streams with an air space above are known as 'Vadose' systems, while for those which are completely waterlogged the term 'phreatic' is used. Caves of both types which are now drained of the streams that formed them are described as 'fossil' systems. Most of the chalk caves so far discovered in Kent and Sussex fall into the 'fossil phreatic' category.

Caves can also form when large masses of rock resting on unstable clay simply move apart, leaving what is in effect a large crack. These are known as 'tectonic' or fissure caves and are often associated with landslips. A good example in chalk is Beachy Head Fissure near the lighthouse (TV584952), situated on the cliff top above a landslip. It consists of a 50ft shaft leading to a tall natural passage, descending to a depth of about 70ft. Similar caves in sandstone occur at Cowden (TQ4941) and behind the fishing huts at Hastings (TQ8309). The well-known Ightham Fissures in Kentish Ragstone (TQ5957) were also probably formed in this way.

A number of streams in S.E. England sink underground in what are generally referred to as sinkholes, swallets or swallow holes and these features have often been used as evidence of cave development in chalk. The best-known example is at North Mimms in Hertfordshire (TL232044) where the Mymmshall Brook sinks into the chalk and has been traced by dye tests to springs up to 11 miles away. Good examples also occur in Kent at Lower Ensden near Chartham (TR0756) where several streams draining off the clay sink into large swallets, up to 60ft wide and 40ft deep at the clay/chalk boundary. One of these holes has a cave mouth at the bottom but it is blocked after a few yards. An interesting recent development was the discovery of a natural chalk cave system in a previously unrecorded swallet at Warren Row in Berkshire (SU8180). The Lower Ensden swallets are almost identical to the Warren Row example and in some cases are considerably larger and take a lot more water.

It is also encouraging to know that the French have been searching for caves in the chalk region of the Paris Basin, which is actually the continuation of the North and South Downs on the other side of the Channel. In spite of 'expert' predictions that any such caves would be small and uninteresting, they have explored numerous examples of up to 2 kilometres in length. Nearly all these French caves were found in wells and this has led to speculation that the underground streamways were located by water divining. On one occasion, the Water Services of Paris are said to have asked a dowser to indicate the exact point at which to dig a well. Their engineer was not convinced, however, and decided to sink a 90ft shaft to one side of the point indicated. At a depth of 60ft there was no sign of water so they dug a tunnel in the direction shown by the dowser — here they met the course of an underground river.

Early Geological Survey publications and natural history journals contain several interesting references to similar caves in Kent. In 1879 workmen digging a tunnel from a well at Strood Waterworks (TQ729693) broke into a large natural cavern containing running water, which was eventually explored for about 200ft. Another reference in 1907 described a cave in a well at Knockholt (TQ483597) which measured 30ft long, 18ft high and 12ft wide with a stream flowing through it. A similar cave and watercourse is said to have been entered at a well near Chatham (TQ776663) and three separate caves were discovered at Blackheath (TQ3877) during the construction of a sewer tunnel. Unfortunately, none of these early finds are accessible today.

More recently, the search for chalk caves has concentrated on the sea cliffs. In addition to the sea caves, there are many cavities at various heights in the cliffs which cannot have resulted from marine erosion. Some of these are infilled with rubble or sediment but others are open cavities large enough to enter. Most of these cavities are inaccessible but some examples near the base of the cliffs have been explored. These include Canterbury Cave and Beachy Head Cave, the latter extending for well over 1,000ft.

Another rock which might conceivably contain caves is the sandy limestone known as 'Kentish Rag'. The River Loose near Maidstone flows underground in this rock for a distance of a quarter of a mile at Boughton Quarries (TQ779516) and, although the valley has been altered by artificial landscaping and quarrying at its sides, the disappearance of the stream appears to result from natural causes. There are also three very powerful springs emerging from the ragstone near West Malling (TQ6757, TQ6956 & TQ7056) and the volume of the water is such that it suggests streams flowing in open cavities rather than seepage through porous rock.

Natural caves can also form in gypsum. This rock does not outcrop at the surface but it is extensively mined at Brightling and Mountfield (see GYPSUM MINES). Conversation with some of the miners seems to confirm that natural caves have been encountered and the miners refer to these caves as 'washouts'.

Canterbury Cave

The entrance to this cave lies on the south side of St Margaret's Bay (TR368442), just above the high water mark. The name 'Canterbury Cave' first appears on a map of the South Forland in 1960 and it is apparently a local name for the cave. At that time it was presumed to be a sea cave and it was not until 1975, when it was examined and surveyed by members of Chelsea Speleological Society, that its true significance was realised. It soon became obvious that the cave could not have resulted from marine erosion as it was above the normal range of the tides and quite extensive. What had happened is that the cliff had exposed a fossil cave system originally formed by an underground stream.

The entrance is a large recess behind a pile of boulders which have fallen from the cliff face (Fig. 30). At the rear of this opening, a passage averaging 7ft wide x 4ft high extends into the cliff in a N.W. direction. About 80ft from the entrance, the passage bends to the right and opens into a small chamber 30ft long x 12ft wide x 5ft high, before resuming its original direction after a sharp left turn. The roof and walls of the chamber have a pitted, sponge-like appearance which is characteristic of a cave originally formed under 'phreatic' conditions when the passage was completely filled with water.

About 50ft beyond this chamber, the passage veers to the left and becomes a flat out crawl for about 20ft. The crawl ends at a T-junction with a roomier passage trending north and the obvious way on is to the right. After crawling over and around boulders for a further 70ft, the cave appears to end in an impenetrable fissure, but closer inspection reveals a low opening on the left hand side. This leads to another stretch of roomier passage, the end of which is choked with rubble and boulders just over 300ft from the entrance.

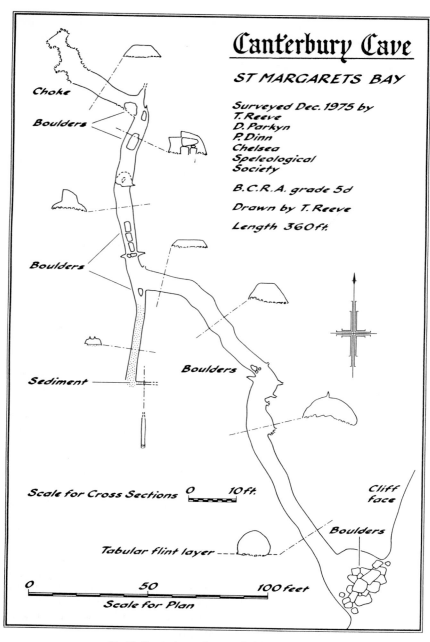

Canterbury Cave

ST MARGARETS BAY

Surveyed Dec. 1975 by
T. Reeve
D. Parkyn
P. Dinn
Chelsea
Speleological
Society

B.C.R.A. grade 5d

Drawn by T. Reeve

Length 360 ft.

Choke

Boulders

Boulders

Sediment

Boulders

Scale for Cross Sections 0 _____ 10 ft.

Cliff
face

Boulders

Tabular flint layer

0 _____ 50 _____ 100 feet
Scale for Plan

Fig.30 Canterbury Cave — St Margaret's Bay

100

To the left of the T-junction, the passage continues southwards but rapidly diminishes in size and is almost choked with sediment, apparently derived from the Thanet Sand which overlies the chalk in some areas. The passage was eventually explored in this direction for about 45ft by digging out the floor and, during the excavation, a number of rat and rabbit bones were unearthed. At the furthest point a small fissure branches off to the left but the way ahead is completely blocked.

The total length of explored passages is 360ft. The passages are clearly joint-orientated but there is another less obvious feature that may have had a considerable influence on the development of the cave, i.e. the thin sheet of tabular flint seen beneath the floor near the entrance. In the cliff face nearby, the chalk above the upper surface of the flint is honeycombed with tiny cavities only a few inches wide. It is interesting to note that the cross sections of the cave discovered at Strood Waterworks also show a flint seam at floor level. Further examples of caves floored with tabular flint can be seen in the cliffs at Beachy Head. These flint layers probably form an effective water barrier which results in a saturated (phreatic) zone above the normal level of the water table. Water held up in this way must eventually drain away, following any incline in the strata or leaking into unsaturated rock below wherever the continuity of the flint is interrupted by faulting, etc. This would result in significant underground water movements, particularly along the joint structure on the upper surface of the flint.

Beachy Head Cave

This is one of the several caves situated in the spectacular chalk cliffs at Beachy Head near Eastbourne (TV578953). The entrance lies in a particularly inaccessible location near the base of a 300ft vertical cliff and involves a difficult climb to a ledge 14ft above the beach. This ledge is actually an exposed bend in a cave passage with two low, semi-circular openings leading off into the cliff. The cave was eventually explored and surveyed (Fig. 29) by members of Chelsea Speleological Society during 6 visits in 1980. Careful planning was required to avoid being cut off by the tide!

To the right of the ledge, the passage extends for 585ft and ends at a 'sump' where it continues full of water. The cave passages are very small and progress is slow — mainly flat out crawling with only occasional sitting or standing space. The floor is either covered with dried out mud or littered with flint nodules, and the whole place is literally crawling with fauna — spiders, gnats, moths, etc. The passage follows the joint network of the chalk with many sharp bends but maintains an overall trend in a N.E. direction away from the cliff face. There are several small tributary passages, including a tube-like opening in the roof which can be climbed to a height of 25ft.

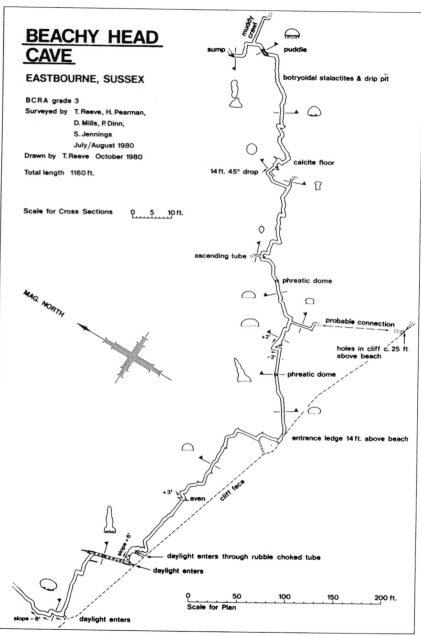

Fig.29 Beachy Head Cave — Eastbourne, Sussex

Flowstone formations in Beachy Head Cave.   (T. Reeve)

The only significant change in the character of the main passage is a curious 14ft drop down a perfectly circular tube inclined at 45 degrees. Beyond this, the previously dry and dusty cave suddenly becomes very damp with slimy black deposits on the walls and puddles spreading across the floor towards the end. It is in this damp section that the only cave formations are seen — some small but attractive crystals and a 'botryoidal' stalactite resembling a cauliflower.

The left hand passage is initially very similar to the right hand series. It extends for 465ft and nearly touches the cliff again in three places where daylight enters from tiny tube-like openings. The passage beyond the second point of daylight penetration is noticeably different from the rest of the cave, formed along a fault with a boulder strewn floor and plenty of standing space. This is followed by two very tight crawls, beyond which the passage steadily increases in size until it is 6ft wide x 5ft high before heading downhill through a series of S-bends. At the bottom of this slope, another very tight crawl leads to a mud-floored passage with the channel of a tiny dried up stream down one side. The passage finally ends where the sediment comes to within a few inches of the roof but it could probably be extended by digging.

As in the caves at Strood and St Margaret's Bay, the cave is formed above a thin tabular flint layer and sudden changes in the level of the passages seem to coincide with displacement of the flint by faulting.

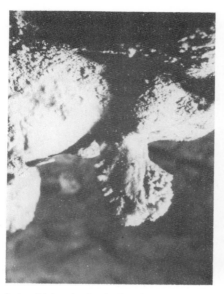 

Botryoidal stalactite in Beachy Head Cave. (T. Reeve)

Cave chamber in chalk. (T. Reeve)

The total length of explored passages is 1,160ft, which makes it the longest so far discovered in the English chalk, and the depth below surface is 300 – 400ft. It is now one of the 50 caves in Britain scheduled as Sites of Special Scientific Interest. Since the cave was surveyed, some spectacular cliff falls have created two new entrances in the left hand series. The original entrance ledge has also collapsed, effectively splitting the cave into two.

Kingsgate Sea Caves

The chalk cliffs of the Isle of Thanet originally contained over 100 caves but most of these have now been destroyed by the construction of sea defences. Some of the best remaining examples are situated in the relatively unspoilt cliffs of the Kingsgate area where various paths and steps provide easy access to the beach at low tide. The largest cave in this area is 'Smugglers Cave' (TR396708) situated in Kingsgate Bay behind the Captain Digby pub. This is over 200ft long x 30ft high but has obviously been artificially enlarged with a high level side passage and blocked shaft at the end, which originally led to the surface. Nearby is the entrance to 'Tower Cave' which is entirely natural and extends for about 100ft.

At the western end of the bay, the headland known as Whiteness Point (TR396710) is pierced by a natural sea cave and a system of man-made tunnels. One of the tunnel entrances is accessible at high tide and a hole in the floor provides a spectacular view of the sea cave below, especially during rough seas. A sketch of this area made by Mr R. Staniforth in 1960 shows these tunnels but not the sea cave, so presumably it did not exist at that time. The rate of erosion is certainly extremely rapid as it has taken less than 30 years for the sea cave to penetrate the 70ft wide headland. Eventually it will collapse and form an isolated stack, similar to those in the adjoining Botany Bay area (TR393711). None of the other caves in the area shows any significant changes since Staniforth made his sketches but a natural arch in Botany Bay has collapsed to form a new offshore stack.

Archaeology & Palaeontology

There are three locations in Kent which have provided interesting finds relating to the late Pleistocene period some 50,000 – 100,000 years ago. The well-known 'rock shelters' at Ightham (TQ585563) are small natural caves and overhangs which occur in the sandstone crags along the eastern edge of Oldbury Hill (Fig. 31). Many interesting features, including at least one fairly substantial cave, have unfortunately been destroyed by quarrying of the outcrops during the early 19th century. The main group of rock shelters surviving today consists of 8 low openings beneath overhanging rocks, some of which interconnect in the form of a small but quite complex cave system with over 150ft of passages. The caves occur in a soft, silty layer sandwiched between hard chert, which forms the roof, and harder sandstone below. They appear to have resulted from differential weathering of the rock outcrops and erosion by springs. It is interesting to note that a small stream rises from a spring at a similar level on the northern side of the hill.

In 1890 a local archaeologist, Benjamin Harrison, directed an excavation which resulted in the discovery of a large collection of Palaeolithic (early Stone Age) flint implements. These were recognised as 'cave dwelling types' almost identical to those found at Le Moustier in France. Unfortunately, there is considerable confusion as to the location of these finds.

A more recent excavation by Desmond and Anne Collins (1965) failed to find any evidence of occupation in the immediate vicinity of the surviving rock shelters but, further down the hillside, more examples of the distinctive 'Mousterian' implements were found. They concluded that, whilst there was no definite evidence of occupation of the shelters in their present-day form, it was possible that the implements were associated with a former rock shelter now destroyed by natural erosion

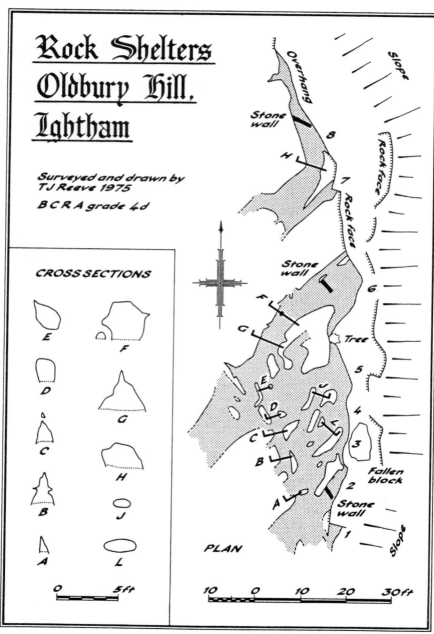

Fig.31 Rock Shelters — Oldbury Hill, Ightham

Oldbury Hill caves.   (M. Jack)

or quarrying. Further excavations could throw more light on the subject but there would seem to be little doubt that it was the shelter provided by the natural caves and overrhangs that attracted the Palaeolithic tool makers to this area some 50,000 years ago.

Another interesting site near Ightham was the 'Ightham Fissures' (TQ5957), discovered and subsequently destroyed by quarrying in the years preceding 1894. A photograph of the site in Bennet's book titled 'Ightham' shows three narrow openings in a ragstone quarry, the largest about 3ft wide. What made these features particularly interesting was the wealth of Pleistocene fossils found inside. The remains comprised 27 land snails, 47 mammals, 3 reptiles, 2 amphibians and 20 birds. The mammals included mammoth, woolly rhinoceros, brown bear, reindeer, red deer, roe deer, horse, wolf, hyena, wild boar, badger, common and arctic fox, otter, weasel, polecat, pika, pouched marmot, mole, shrew, field mouse, 5 species of bat and several species of vole and lemming. It will be seen that some of these animals are now extinct or no longer present in the British Isles, whilst others are still common species today.

There are also references to a 'Boughton Cave' near Maidstone (TQ7852) where the remains of mammoth, woolly rhinoceros, reindeer and red deer were found.

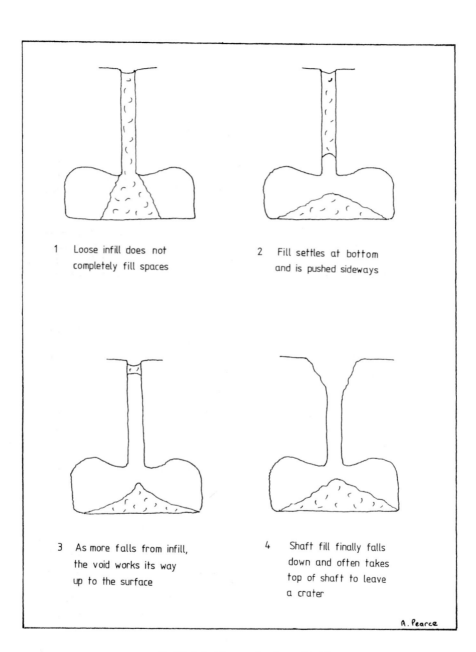

1   Loose infill does not completely fill spaces

2   Fill settles at bottom and is pushed sideways

3   As more falls from infill, the void works its way up to the surface

4   Shaft fill finally falls down and often takes top of shaft to leave a crater

A. Pearce

Fig.32 Subsidence: Settling of infill

Subsidence

From the previous pages the reader will have realised the extent of underground spaces in Kent and Sussex. Considering the number of such sites, the actual instances of ground subsidence are fortunately small, but this is little consolation to the person whose field or garden collapses. It is a traumatic experience and there has been a tendency in the past to adopt the principle of 'out of sight, out of mind' and to quickly fill in the hole with rubble. This, however, is a short-sighted view since the subsidence can happen again in the future! The correct treatment of subsidence depends on the cause and there are four main reasons why it happens.

Settling of Infill

Throwing loosely-compacted rubble or other rubbish into a hole can fill it up quickly but this is only short term. After a few years, items like wood, etc. can rot and the weight of infill causes loose rubble to become compacted. This causes settling of the infill and it often happens that a large void is formed (Fig. 32), not necessarily continued to the surface. If there are side chambers or passages, the weight of infill causes the bottom part to be pushed sideways into the spaces and this again leaves a large void. Over the years, the void gradually works its way upwards as more infill falls into the space until just a thin 'crust' is left at the surface. This can suddenly collapse under its own weight or, even worse, under the weight of a person or vehicle passing over it.

Collapse of Steining

Old wells (and sometimes deneholes) were walled around at the top by bricks or flints called 'steining'. Until solid chalk was reached, this was necessary to stop surrounding soil, etc. from collapsing into the shaft. Many such features have been covered over in the past without filling the shaft itself but, over the years, the bricks or flints can fall away leaving the steining in a weakened condition (Fig. 33). This can be aggravated if the feature has been adapted as a cesspit or land drain, since the water falling down the sides erodes the mortar and bricks. Once the steining falls away, the surrounding soil collapses into the shaft and a large crater is formed which can undermine any covering, causing it to fall into the shaft.

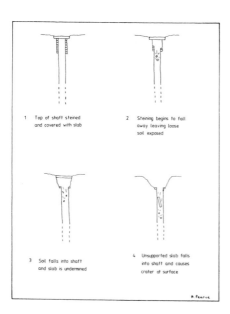

Fig.33 Subsidence: Collapse of steining

1 Top of shaft steined and covered with slab

2 Steining begins to fall away leaving loose soil exposed

3 Soil falls into shaft and slab is undermined

4 Unsupported slab falls into shaft and causes crater at surface

R. Pearce

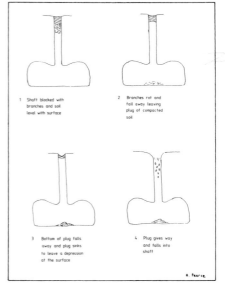

1 Shaft blocked with branches and soil level with surface

2 Branches rot and fall away leaving plug of compacted soil

3 Bottom of plug falls away and plug sinks to leave a depression at the surface

4 Plug gives way and falls into shaft

R. Pearce

Fig.34 Subsidence: Slippage of blockage

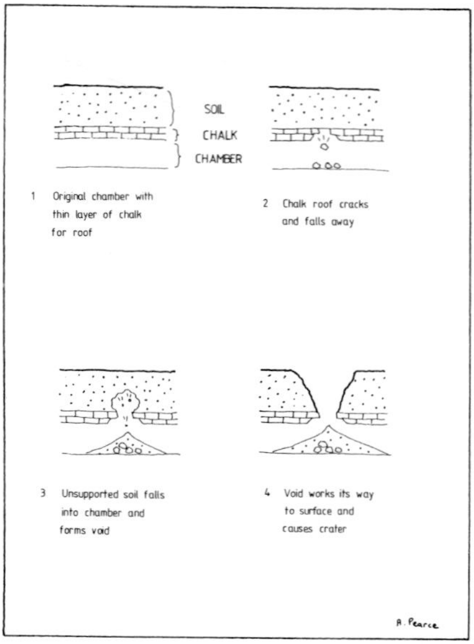

SOIL
CHALK
CHAMBER

1 Original chamber with thin layer of chalk for roof

2 Chalk roof cracks and falls away

3 Unsupported soil falls into chamber and forms void

4 Void works its way to surface and causes crater

R. Pearce

Fig.35 Subsidence: Chamber collapse

110

Slippage of Shaft Blockage

Many deneholes were not infilled upon abandonment but were blocked a few feet down by throwing in branches and tree trunks. Flints and soil were then thrown in to fill the shaft to the surface level. This may seem a risky method to us but we should remember that deneholes were sunk along field boundaries or in small copses and the landowners knew exactly where they were. Over the years, however, land changes hands and the locations are forgotton. Nowadays, many of these field boundaries have been removed to make larger fields or housing sites and this is one of the most common causes of subsidence in Kent. The original blockage has rotted away over the years and the soil layer now forms a compacted plug at the top (Fig. 34). During alternating periods of dry and wet weather, the plug contracts and expands which causes it to slip slowly down the shaft (this explains many of the hollows found in woods). After a particularly heavy rain, the plug may suddenly disintegrate completely and fall down the shaft, especially if it is assisted by the vibration of agricultural machinery or the increased weight of high density housing.

Chamber Collapse

The chambers excavated for deneholes or chalk mines are quite high and the roof level is usually just below the top of the chalk strata. Unless particular care was taken in shaping the roof the chalk has a tendency to crack and, being unsupported, will fall into the chamber below (Fig. 35). This process can be accelerated if the chamber is at a shallow depth and extra weight is placed at the surface, e.g. a house, road, etc. Once the chalk layer has disappeared, the overlying strata is exposed and also begins to fall into the chamber below. This is especially so with Thanet Sand since wet weather will quickly cause draining water to erode the sides of a void. The void works its way up to the surface and falling material cannot block the void since it rolls sideways into the chamber below. As soon as the void reaches the surface, it appears as a spectacular crater. A similar effect can happen in natural cave chambers in chalk when the chamber becomes so big that it is no longer stable.

Treatment

The best treatment is obviously preventative and more care should be taken in checking ground cleared for housing or larger fields. Members of the Kent Underground Research Group can advise on the likely existence of such problems and a computerised database of all known underground sites in the South East is maintained. If it is too late, then it is vital to find the cause of the subsidence before treating it and the Group can also assist with this. They can carry out an underground survey which will indicate if there are other likely danger points. As a rule of thumb, it can be stated that loose rubble infills alone must never be used since they will not be a permanent solution.

If the subsidence has caused a large crater, then it is likely that the only treatment is a complete infill. This must be done in such a way that ALL voids are filled and it is necessary to use a material that can flow into every crevice and then set hard. The ideal material is Pulverised Fuel Ash (PFA) which is the waste product from power stations. This is mixed into a slurry and poured into the hole, where it spreads to fill every void and sets as hard as concrete. If the underground system is extensive, such as a chalk mine, then an alternative solution may be required since the quantities of PFA would be extremely expensive. In such cases, the best solution is to strengthen weak points of the roof with rock bolts, steel mesh and sprayed on concrete. The mine passages themselves can be left open with permanent access to check on the condition of the roof.

If a subsidence reveals that a shaft is still reasonably intact, there are two alternative solutions to a complete infill if the bottom chambers are stable. All that is required is to replace any missing steining and re-mortar it at the top. A concrete cap can then be installed over the shaft, below ground level if necessary, making sure that it extends at least 3ft beyond the shaft edges all round. If an access lid is incorporated, this will allow future checks to be carried out for stability. Instead of a concrete cap, a hinged metal grid can also be used, which will make the feature safe but will allow people to look down and perhaps allow access for bats. It could become a feature of the garden! With such methods, it is not advisable to continue using the shaft as a drain but, if this is necessary, any pipe should direct water down the centre of the shaft rather than the sides.

If access is not required, then a cheap alternative is a mixture of the two methods. The shaft can be filled with rubble to within 15ft of the top and the steining re-pointed. The last 15ft is then filled with PFA which is also carried on for 1ft above the shaft top and 3ft to the sides. The PFA sets to form a plug which will then remain, even if the the rubble settles below. The plug can be further secured by inserting a number of horizontal bars into the shaft sides before filling with PFA.

Cave Wildlife

Despite the absence of light, a variety of plants and animals are to be found underground and, although there are both natural and man-made sites, for the purposes of this section the term 'cave' will be used as an overall description. Not all parts of the cave are totally dark and it is usually divided into three distinct zones, viz:

ENTRANCE ZONE — the actual entrance to a tunnel or shaft which receives a normal amount of light.

THRESHOLD ZONE — the area inside the cave which still receives some light, however little. It also includes the base of a shaft where accidental cave dwellers can be found.

DARK ZONE — the area which never receives any light at all.

The presence (or absence) of light can determine the type of plant or animal that inhabits a particular place in a cave but there are also other factors such as temperature, air flow, humidity, food supply and even the time of year. There are three main groups of animals that inhabit caves, viz:

TROGLOBITE — an animal that lives permanently in a cave and is never found on the surface.

TROGLOPHILE — an animal that usually lives in a cave but can also be found on the surface.

TROGLOXENE — an animal that regularly uses a cave for part of its life (one or two members of Kent Underground Research Group come into this category!). Most trogloxenes use a cave during winter for the purposes of shelter or hibernation.

Unlike their surface relatives, very little research has been carried out on cave animals and the one thing we know about them is that we do not know very much at all! Members of the Group are carrying out research and would appreciate details of any sightings of plants or animals found in caves. The examples which follow are the ones most likely to be found in Kent and Sussex. The common name has been used where possible but the Latin name appears where there is no other.

FUNGUS GNAT — this small fly has a humped thorax and small spines on the leg joints. It is the nearest we have to a troglobite as its complete life cycle is spent underground. The white, dark-headed larva lives on minute fungi growing on cave walls and the pupa hangs from the roof before changing into a gnat. The only reason it cannot be called a true troglobite is because it can be found above ground, although possibly inhabiting animal burrows, holes in trees

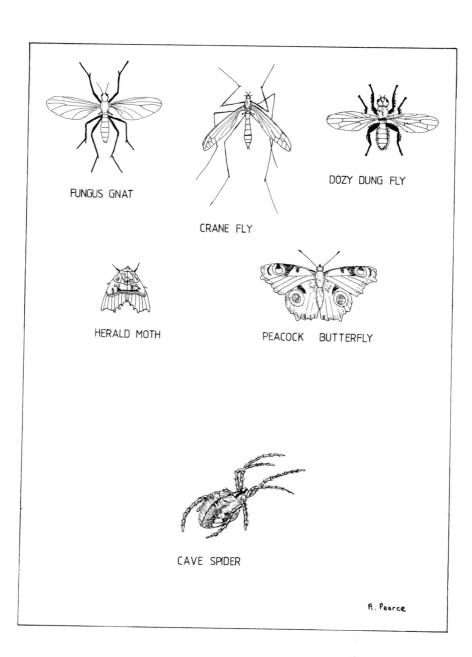

FUNGUS GNAT

CRANE FLY

DOZY DUNG FLY

HERALD MOTH

PEACOCK BUTTERFLY

CAVE SPIDER

A. Pearce

Fig.36 Cave Insects and Spiders

and cracks in rocks. It is very difficult to identify since there are about 500 different species of fungus gnat, although only a few are found underground.

FLIES — In winter, animals resembling bees can sometimes be found hibernating in tiny holes in cave walls. These are actually harmless Drone Flies which rely on their resemblance to honey bee drones for protection. They breed on the surface and the larva is the 'rat-tailed maggot' found in stagnant water. During summer, several other species of fly can be found resting on cave walls such as the Caddis Fly and Crane Fly. It is still not known why they undergo this resting stage in their life cycle without food.

MOTHS — The Tissue Moth and Herald Moth can often be found hibernating in the threshold and dark zones of a cave, sometimes so covered with droplets of condensation that they can hardly be seen. The larvae of both species are surface dwellers and it seems to be only the adults which venture underground. The Herald Moth has been known to spend up to 10 months in a cave and, since this cannot be solely hibernation, more research is needed to investigate this part of its life cycle.

BUTTERFLIES — Most species hibernate on the surface in the egg, larva or pupa stage but some can be found in the threshold zone hibernating as adults. The most common species is the Peacock but the Small Tortoiseshell and Comma are also found. The Red Admiral and Painted Lady have been found trying to hibernate but there is no evidence of them succeeding, although they could possibly do so during a mild winter.

SPIDERS — The species known as *Meta merianae* can be found in the entrance and threshold zones but its close relative, *Meta menardi*, is a true cave spider from the dark zone. This is an attractive, shiny-looking spider and its egg sacs can often be seen hanging from the roof. In recent years, experts have found a slightly different variety called *Meta bourneti* but it is very difficult to tell them apart.

FOXES — A sand mine at Greenwich is home to a number of foxes which leave their distinctive smell and droppings as evidence. Where the roof falls prevent us from going any further, the foxes have made their own system of tunnels into what must be a very extensive and safe lair.

BATS — Over the last 50 years the bat population of Britain has declined drastically and this is believed to have been caused by modern farming methods, use of pesticides and disturbance of their roosting/hibernation sites. Some species, such as the Horseshoe Bats, have disappeared completely from Kent and Sussex where they were once common. Caves are very important to many species of bat and, although breeding roosts are usually on the surface, one mine in Kent is known to be used occasionally for this purpose. Mating occurs in autumn but fertilization is delayed until the spring, with only one offspring a year except for occasional twins. With declining numbers, it is important that each rearing is successful and any disturbance during this period is critical.

During winter their food supply declines and this means that bats have to hibernate to survive until spring. In late autumn they put on weight so that their fat reserves will last them for up to five months of hibernation, during which time their body temperature drops to nearly zero and their metabolism slows right down. Caves are used by many species for hibernation but only where the air flow, humidity and temperature are fairly constant. Bats can detect quite minute changes and will wake up to change their position in a cave or even fly to another site. Once a suitable cave site has been found, they crawl into a crevice (only some species hang upside down) and this is when problems can occur.

If they are disturbed, they slowly wake up as the body temperature rises and this uses up a surprising amount of energy. The heartbeat increases from 25 beats a minute to 1,000 when in flight and the valuable fat reserves are depleted with little hope of replenishment. Too many disturbances will mean that the fat reserves will not last the winter and they literally starve to death. In a state of hibernation, bats are so torpid that they appear dead, but it takes very little to disturb them. Shining bright lights on the bats or even the heat of a person's body in a confined space is sufficient to wake them up. It is thus vital that anyone finding a bat underground leaves immediately.

Bats are now a protected species under the Wildlife and Country-side Act 1981 and it is an offence to knowingly disturb a hibernating bat or block up the entrance to a roost. Special licences are granted by the Nature Conservancy Council to conservationists who monitor bat sites and even they are not allowed to visit sites more than three times over winter. The bat workers are part of a national group of volunteers who are building up a picture of the needs of bats so that ways can be found to help them. They work closely with groups such as KURG who use their equipment and expertise to take them into the underground sites. A voluntary code of practice has now been introduced to restrict winter visits to sites used by bats and it has been found that the reduced disturbance allows the bat population to increase. A particularly important site at the Westerham Ragstone Mine is gated and access strictly controlled.

The bat species found in this area are Brandts, Brown, Long Eared, Daubenton's, Natterer's, Pipistrelle and Whiskered. The KURG has a Bat Liaison Officer and he would welcome details of any sighting of bats underground. If you did not know in advance that bats were present at a site, you have no reason to worry about breaking the law so long as you leave the site immediately. Further details of bats and Bat Groups can be obtained by writing to KURG who will pass on the query.

FUNGI — The lack of light means that ordinary plants cannot survive in caves. Fungi, however, are perfectly equipped to live in the dark since they do not have chlorophyll and do not need light to manufacture food. They reproduce by spores and, when blown by the slightest current of air, will immediately start growing when they land on anything organic. This can be pit props, pieces of wood, dead insects, bat droppings or even an explorer's discarded sandwich. They secrete enzymes which break down the organic material and this is absorbed by the plant. Some species send out long, thread-like filaments which, if they come across another food source, will break and form a separate plant. Some mines in Britain have been used to grow mushrooms commercially but, for some reason, attempts in the South East have never been successful.

Some underground fungi can grow into marvellous shapes and there are many different colours, the latter depending on the food source. One species hangs down from pit props to form a threadlike curtain and another forms jelly-like stalactites. In the Greenwich sand mine, a species grows on the fox droppings with thin filaments that stand upright. The most common form in Kent and Sussex sends out horizontal filaments similar to a spider's web and these can sometimes cover the whole floor. Very little research has been carried out into cave fungi and identification is a specialist art. There are thousands of species of fungi in Britain and some adopt completely different shapes when growing underground.

Bibliography

(All can be ordered via your local library, but most are out of print so can only be bought if you can find a copy in a secondhand bookshop.)

CHELSEA SPELEOLOGICAL SOCIETY RECORDS. ISSN 0309 409X
'Deneholes' 1965, Editor H. Pearman
'Caves & Tunnels in Kent' 1973, Editor H. Pearman
'Caves & Tunnels in S.E. England, Pt.1' 1976, Editor H. Pearman
'Caves & Tunnels in S.E. England, Pt.2' 1978, Editor H. Pearman
'Caves & Tunnels in S.E. England, Pt.3' 1979, Editor T. Reeve
'Deneholes Pt.2' 1979, Editor R.F. Le Gear
'Caves & Tunnels in S.E. England, Pt.4' 1982, Editor H. Pearman
'Underground Gazetteer of S.E. England' 1983, Editor H. Pearman
'Caves & Tunnels in S.E. England, Pt.5' 1983, Editor H. Pearman
'Caves & Tunnels in S.E. England, Pt.6' 1984, Editor H. Pearman
'Caves & Tunnels in S.E. England, Pt.7' 1987, Editor H. Pearman
'Caves & Tunnels in S.E. England, Pt.8' 1988, Editor H. Pearman

CLEERE, H. & CROSSLEY, D. 'Iron Industry of the Weald' 1985, Leicester University Press. ISBN 0 718512 13 8.

COBBETT, W. 'Rural Rides — Counties of Kent & Sussex' 1893.

KENT UNDERGROUND RESEARCH GROUP. ISSN 0953 0819
'Deneholes in the Gravesend Area' 1984, R.F. Le Gear
'RACS Chalk Mine' 1987, R.F. Le Gear
'Chalk Mining in Frindsbury' 1987, A.J. Pearce & D. Long
'Annual Research Report' 1987, Editor A.J. Pearce
'Annual Research Report' 1988, Editor A.J. Pearce

HILTON, J. 'History of the Kent Coalfield' 1986, ISBN X 860906 05 0

MANTELL, G.A. 'Geology of the S.E. of England' 1833.

RITCHIE, A.E. 'The Kent Coalfield' 1919, Iron & Coal Trades Review.

SHEPHERD, R. 'Prehistoric Mining & Allied Industries' 1980, London Academic Press, ISBN 0 126394 80 6.

STRAKER, E. 'Wealden Iron' 1969, David & Charles, ISBN 0 715344 70 6.

TOPLEY, W. 'Geology of the Weald' 1875, HMSO.

WELBY, J. 'Dover's Forgotten Fortress', Kent County Library, ISBN 0 905155 43 2.

WHITAKER, W. 'Water Supply of Kent' 1908, HMSO.

WHITAKER, W. 'Water Supply of Sussex' 1899, HMSO.

WILLMOTT, F.G. 'Bricks & Brickies' 1972, Meresborough Books, ISBN 0 905270 01 0.

YOUNG, A. 'General View of the Agriculture of the County of Sussex' 1813, Sherwood, Neely & Jones.

In addition to the above, your reference library can supply the local geological memoir and old Ordnance Survey 25":1 mile maps, which show much detail now missing from modern maps. The latter will be dated around 1870, 1890, 1910 and 1938. Advice on further references can be obtained by sending a SAE to KURG.

Glossary of Terms

ADIT — horizontal mine entrance or access passage.
BACKFILL — to fill an abandoned mine cavity with waste rock.
BED — layer of rock in the ground.
BELLPIT — shallow shaft with one or two chambers at bottom.
BOREHOLE (1) — hole drilled with a hollow tube that removes sections of rock for identification.
          (2) — narrow hole sunk as a water supply.
CAP — covering to a shaft.
CAVE — natural cavity.
CHAMBER — underground cavity either natural or mined.
CONDUIT — underground passage for conducting water.
CROSS CUT — access passage linking two parallel adits.
DAY FALL — where mine workings have collapsed at the surface.
DIP — angle at which strata differs from the horizontal.
DRIFT — same as ADIT.
FACE — furthest working part of a mine.
FAULT — large fissure which displaces strata.
GALLERY — horizontal working area in coal or iron mine.
GROTTO — artificially decorated chamber.
GRUB — to remove woods or field boundaries.
INFILL — material thrown into a shaft to fill it up.
JOINT — fissure in rock, especially chalk.
KILN — structure which roasts chalk or limestone to make lime.
KNAPPING — to hit a flint so that flakes break off.
LEVEL — same as ADIT.
MINE — cavity excavated to extract rock or mineral.
MINE AGENT — man in charge of a mine.
ORE — rock in which a metal occurs.
OUTCROP — point where strata is exposed at the surface.
PILLAR — section of rock left to support the roof.
ROCK SHELTER — small cavity in a cliff face.
SALLY PORT — door for defenders to make surprise attacks from.
SEAM — layer of coal or iron in the ground.

SHAFT — vertical entrance to a mine or well. Separate shafts can be sunk for pumping, ventilation or winding up rock.

SMELTING — process of roasting ore to product metal.

SPOIL — waste rock brought to the surface and left in heaps.

STEINING — shaft or well lining made of bricks or flints.

STRATA — same as BED.

SUMP (1) — drainage hole at the base of a shaft
  (2) — cave passage flooded to the roof.

TIMBERING — wooden roof props in levels or walls in shafts.

TRAMWAY — rails laid for waggons to be pushed along.

TUB — mine waggon.

UNDERCUT — to excavate underneath rock so that it falls down.

VEIN — underground deposit, usually of ore.

WINDLASS — small hand winch for winding in shafts.

WORKINGS — general term for all mine passages.

Index

The Authors

JIM BRADSHAW has been involved in many aspects of archaeology and has supervised several excavations. With a few others, he carried out a comprehensive survey of deneholes in East Kent and is the acknowledged expert on this area. He is a past council member of Kent Archaeological Society and a retired forester.

NESTA CAIGER assisted her husband John in denehole research in the 1950s when much valuable information was obtained. She is interested in many aspects of archaeology and is an expert in domestic features such as icewells, cesspits, etc. She is a council member of Kent Archaeological Society and now retired.

MIKE HALPIN is interested both in the archaeology and natural history of underground features. His speciality is research into underground sites used by hibernating bats as well as insects and his many wanderings have uncovered sites in out of the way places. He runs his own cleaning business.

ROD LE GEAR has been involved in the archaeology of underground sites since the 1960s and was the prime mover in forming the KURG. He is the expert on deneholes in N.W. Kent as well as several chalk mines. He is a council member of Kent Archaeological Society and a senior engineer with Rank Xerox.

ADRIAN PEARCE has been exploring and researching mines all over the UK for 20 years. He was involved with setting up the National Association of Mining History Organisations and is a past Chairman and Secretary. He works for the Inland Revenue.

HARRY PEARMAN started by caving with Chelsea Speleological Society and also became interested in underground sites in the S.E. He edits the CSS publications on such sites and these have become invaluable as a gazeteer and bibliography for researchers. He is a computer manager for a local authority.

TERRY REEVE was a pioneer in discovering natural chalk caves in the S.E. which many people said could not exist. He has proved them wrong by uncovering large natural systems and has spent many years in surveying such caves as well as deneholes, etc. He works in the Planning Dept of a local authority.

PAUL SOWAN has been involved in exploration of stone mines throughout the UK and Europe for many years. He is a researcher 'par excellence' and his speciality is in uncovering references in obscure publications. He is regarded as the national expert on stone mines and is a teacher in Croydon.

Kent Underground Research Group

The Group is a branch of Kent Archaeological Society and was formed in 1981 to carry out research into the origins, use and history of the many subterranean features of Kent and the South East.

The members are a unique mixture of the practical and academic. On the active side they explore and survey underground features for which they have the necessary skills and equipment. Some projects call for technical expertise in the use of pumps, winches, timbering, etc. Safety is a very big feature in the Group's activities and new members are taught the skills by others with many years' experience. On the academic side, they carry out research into old records as well as talking to elderly residents whose memories are invaluable. All these skills are brought together to publish the history of sites in the Group's Research Reports. Every member has something to contribute regardless of age, ability or fitness.

The Group produces 4 Newsletters and an Annual Research Report each year, free to members. Special Research Reports are occasionally produced on specific subjects where they are large enough to warrant it. There is an Institutional Membership for organisations such as libraries which wish to receive the publications only. Although individual projects are encouraged, the Group organises field meetings during the year to sites of interest as well as social events.

The Group is willing, at short notice, to visit sites where they can advise on the origin and extent of an underground feature. Although they concentrate on Kent, the Group has been called out to places as far away as Sussex and Berkshire. There are a number of Field Officers who carry out the initial visit and, if further work is needed, they will arrange for other members to join them to carry out exploration and surveys.

Requests for assistance or further details of the Group should be sent to the Secretary:

R.F. Le Gear
18 Bladindon Drive
Bexley
Kent DA5 3BP
Tel: 081-304-1781

A self-addressed envelope would be appreciated if a written reply is needed.

Meresborough Books

17 Station Road, Rainham, Gillingham, Kent. ME8 7RS
Telephone: Medway (0634) 388812

We are a specialist publisher of books about Kent. Our books are available in most bookshops in the county, including our own at this address. Alternatively you may order direct, adding 10% for post (minimum 30p, orders over £25 post free). ISBN prefix 0 905270 for 3 figure numbers, 094819 for 4 figure numbers. Titles in print April 1991.

HARDBACKS

AIRCRAFT CASUALTIES IN KENT Part One 1939-40 compiled by G.G. Baxter, K.A. Owen and P. Baldock. ISBN 3506. £12.95.
BARGEBUILDING ON THE SWALE by Don Sattin. ISBN 3530. £9.95.
EDWARDIAN CHISLEHURST by Arthur Battle. ISBN 3433. £9.95.
FISHERMEN FROM THE KENTISH SHORE by Derek Coombe. ISBN 3409. £10.95.
THE GILLS by Tony Conway. ISBN 266. £5.95. BARGAIN OFFER £1.95.
THE HISTORY OF THE ROYAL SEA BATHING HOSPITAL, MARGATE 1791-1991 by F.G. St Clair Strange. ISBN 3573. £12.95.
JUST OFF THE SWALE by Don Sattin. ISBN 045. £5.95.
KENT CASTLES by John Guy. ISBN 150. £7.50.
KENT'S OWN by Robin J. Brooks. The history of 500 (County of Kent) Squadron of the R.A.A.F. ISBN 541. £5.95.
THE LONDON, CHATHAM & DOVER RAILWAY by Adrian Gray. ISBN 886. £7.95.
THE NATURAL HISTORY OF ROMNEY MARSH by Dr F.M. Firth, M.A., Ph.D. ISBN 789. £6.95.
A NEW DICTIONARY OF KENT DIALECT by Alan Major. ISBN 274. £7.50.
THE PAST GLORY OF MILTON CREEK by Alan Cordell and Leslie Williams. ISBN 3042. £9.95.
ROCHESTER FROM OLD PHOTOGRAPHS compiled by the City of Rochester Society. Large format. ISBN 975. £7.95.(Also available in paperback ISBN 983. £4.95.)
SHERLOCK HOLMES AND THE KENT RAILWAYS by Kelvin Jones. ISBN 3255. £8.95.
SOUTH EAST BRITAIN: ETERNAL BATTLEGROUND by Gregory Blaxland. A military history. ISBN 444. £5.95. BARGAIN £2.95.
STRATFORD HOUSE SCHOOL 1912-1987 by Susan Pittman. ISBN 3212. £10.00.
TALES OF VICTORIAN HEADCORN or The Oddities of Heddington by Penelope Rivers (Ellen M. Poole). ISBN 3050. £8.95. (Also available in paperback ISBN 3069. £3.95).
TEYNHAM MANOR AND HUNDRED (798-1935) by Elizabeth Selby, MBE. ISBN 630. £5.95.
TROOPSHIP TO CALAIS by Derek Spiers. ISBN 3395. £11.95.
TWO HALVES OF A LIFE by Doctor Kary Pole. ISBN 509. £5.95.
US BARGEMEN by A.S. Bennett. ISBN 207. £6.95.
A VIEW OF CHRIST'S COLLEGE, BLACKHEATH by A.E.O. Crombie, B.A. ISBN 223. £6.95.

STANDARD SIZE PAPERBACKS

BIRDS OF KENT: A Review of their Status and Distribution by the Kent Ornithological Society. ISBN 800. £6.95.

BIRDWATCHING IN KENT by Don Taylor. ISBN 932. £4.50.

THE CANTERBURY MONSTERS by John H. Vaux. ISBN 3468. £2.50.

THE CHATHAM DOCKYARD STORY by Philip MacDougall. ISBN 3301. £6.95.

CHIDDINGSTONE — AN HISTORICAL EXPLORATION by Jill Newton. ISBN 940. £1.95.

A CHRONOLOGY OF ROCHESTER by Brenda Purle. ISBN 851. £1.50.

COBHAM. Published for Cobham Parish Council. ISBN 3123. £1.00.

CRIME AND CRIMINALS IN VICTORIAN KENT by Adrian Gray. ISBN 967. £3.95.

CURIOUS KENT by John Vigar. ISBN 878. (reprinting)

CYCLE TOURS OF KENT by John Guy. No. 1: Medway, Gravesend, Sittingbourne ·and Sheppey. ISBN 517. £1.50.

EXPLORING KENT CHURCHES by John E. Vigar. ISBN 3018. £3.95.

EXPLORING SUSSEX CHURCHES by John E. Vigar. ISBN 3093. £3.95.

FLIGHT IN KENT. ISBN 3085. £1.95.

FROM MOTHS TO MERLINS: The History of West Malling Airfield by Robin J. Brooks. ISBN 3239. £4.95.

THE GHOSTS OF KENT by Peter Underwood. ISBN 86X. (Reprinting)

A HISTORY OF CHATHAM GRAMMAR SCHOOL FOR GIRLS, 1907-1982 by Audrey Perkyns. ISBN 576. £1.95.

KENT AIRFIELDS IN THE BATTLE OF BRITAIN by the Kent Aviation Historical Research Society. ISBN 3247. (Reprinting)

KENT AND EAST SUSSEX UNDERGROUND by The Kent Underground Research Group. ISBN 3581. £5.95.

KENT COUNTRY CHURCHES by James Antony Syms. ISBN 3131. £4.50.

KENT COUNTRY CHURCHES CONTINUED by James Antony Syms. ISBN 314X. £5.95.

KENT COUNTRY CHURCHES CONCLUDED by James Antony Syms. ISBN 345X. £5.95.

KENT INNS AND SIGNS by Michael David Mirams. ISBN 3182. **BARGAIN £2.50.**

LET'S EXPLORE THE RIVER DARENT by Frederick Wood. ISBN 770. £1.95.

LULLINGSTONE PARK: THE EVOLUTION OF A MEDIAEVAL DEER PARK by Susan Pittman. ISBN 703. £3.95.

PENINSULA ROUND (The Hoo Peninsula) by Des Worsdale. ISBN 568. £1.50.

PRELUDE TO WAR: Aviation in Kent 1938-39 by KAHRS. ISBN 3476. £2.50.

RADIO KENT GARDENERS' GUIDE by Harry Smith and Bob Collard. ISBN 3549. £3.95.

REAL ALE PUBS IN KENT by CAMRA in Kent. ISBN 3263. Was £1.95. Now 95p.

SAINT ANDREW'S CHURCH, DEAL by Gregory Holyoake. ISBN 835. 95p.

SHORNE: The History of a Kentish Village by A.F. Allen. ISBN 3204. £4.95.

SIR GARRARD TYRWHITT-DRAKE AND THE COBTREE ESTATE, MAIDSTONE by Elizabeth Melling B.A. ISBN 3344. £1.50.

SITTINGBOURNE & KEMSLEY LIGHT RAILWAY STOCKBOOK AND GUIDE. ISBN 843. 95p.

STEAM IN MY FAMILY by John Newton. ISBN 3417. £4.95.

STOUR VALLEY WALKS from Canterbury to Sandwich by Christopher Donaldson. ISBN 991. £1.95.

TALES OF VICTORIAN HEADCORN — see under hardbacks.

TARGET FOLKESTONE by Roy Humphreys. ISBN 3514. £7.95.

WADHURST: Town of the High Weald by Alan Savidge and Oliver Mason. ISBN 3352. £5.95.

WARTIME KENT 1939-40 compiled by Oonagh Hyndman from the BBC Radio Kent broadcasts. ISBN 3611. £6.95.

WHERE NO FLOWERS GROW by George Glazebrook. ISBN 3379. £2.50.

WHO'S BURIED WHERE IN KENT by Alan Major. ISBN 3484. £5.95.

LARGE FORMAT PICTORIAL PAPERBACKS

ARE YOU BEING SERVED, MADAM? by Molly Proctor. ISBN 3174. £3.50.

AVIATION IN KENT by Robin J. Brooks. ISBN 681. £2.95.

BEFORE AND AFTER THE HURRICANE IN AND AROUND CANTERBURY by Paul Crampton. ISBN 3387. £3.50. BARGAIN £1.95.

THE BLITZ OF CANTERBURY by Paul Crampton. ISBN 3441. £3.50.

CANTERBURY THEN AND NOW by Paul Crampton. ISBN 359X. £3.95.

EAST KENT FROM THE AIR by John Guy. ISBN 3158. £3.50.

EAST SUSSEX RAILWAYS IN OLD POSTCARDS by Kevin Robertson. ISBN 3220. £3.50.

GEORGE BARGEBRICK Esq. by Richard-Hugh Perks. ISBN 479. £4.50.

HEADCORN: A Pictorial History by the Headcorn Local History Society. ISBN 3271. £3.50.

KENT TOWN CRAFTS by Richard Filmer. ISBN 584. £2.95.

THE LIFE AND ART OF ONE MAN by Dudley Pout. ISBN 525. £2.95.

THE MEDWAY TOWNS FROM THE AIR by Piers Morgan and Diane Nicholls. ISBN 3557. £4.95.

MORE PICTURES OF RAINHAM by Barbara Mackay Miller. ISBN 3298. £3.50.

THE MOTOR BUS SERVICES OF KENT AND EAST SUSSEX — A brief history by Eric Baldock. ISBN 959. £4.95.

OLD BROADSTAIRS by Michael David Mirams. ISBN 3115. £3.50.

OLD CHATHAM: A THIRD PICTURE BOOK by Philip MacDougall. ISBN 3190. £3.50. BARGAIN £1.95.

OLD FAVERSHAM by Arthur Percival. ISBN 3425. £3.50.

OLD GILLINGHAM by Philip MacDougall. ISBN 3328. £3.50.

OLD MAIDSTONE'S PUBLIC HOUSES by Irene Hales. ISBN 533. £2.95. BARGAIN £1.95.

OLD MAIDSTONE Vol.3 by Irene Hales. ISBN 3336. £3.50. BARGAIN £1.95.

OLD MARGATE by Michael David Mirams. ISBN 851. £3.50.

OLD PUBS OF TUNBRIDGE WELLS & DISTRICT by Keith Hetherington and Alun Griffiths. ISBN 300X. £3.50.

OLD RAMSGATE by Michael David Mirams. ISBN 797. £3.50.

PEMBURY IN THE PAST by Mary Standen. ISBN 916. £2.95.

A PICTORIAL STUDY OF ALKHAM PARISH by Susan Lees and Roy Humphreys. ISBN 3034. £2.95.

A PICTORIAL STUDY OF HAWKINGE PARISH by Roy Humphreys. ISBN 328X. £3.50.

A PICTUREBOOK OF OLD NORTHIAM by Lis Rigby. ISBN 3492. £3.95.

A PICTUREBOOK OF OLD RAINHAM by Barbara Mackay Miller. ISBN 606. £3.50.

REMINISCENCES OF OLD CRANBROOK by Joe Woodcock. ISBN 331X. £3.50.

ROCHESTER FROM OLD PHOTOGRAPHS — see under hardbacks.

SMARDEN: A Pictorial History by Jenni Rodger. ISBN 592. £3.50.

THOMAS SIDNEY COOPER OF CANTERBURY by Brian Stewart. ISBN 762. £2.95.

WEST KENT FROM THE AIR by John Guy. ISBN 3166. £3.50.

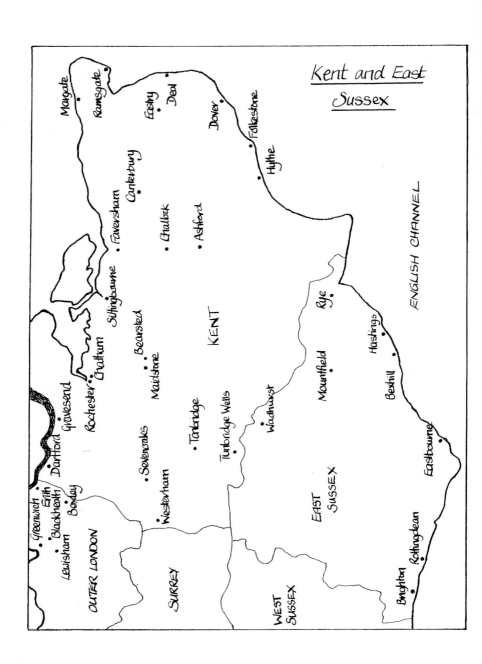

Kent and East Sussex

ENGLISH CHANNEL

Margate
Ramsgate
Eastry
Deal
Dover
Folkestone
Hythe

Canterbury
Faversham
Challock
Ashford

Sittingbourne
Bearsted
KENT
Rye

Gravesend
Chatham
Rochester
Maidstone
Hastings

Dartford
Sevenoaks
Tonbridge
Tunbridge Wells
Wadhurst
Mountfield
Bexhill

Greenwich
Erith
Blackheath
Bexley
Westerham
Eastbourne

Lewisham
OUTER LONDON

SURREY

WEST SUSSEX

EAST SUSSEX

Brighton
Rottingdean